Advance Praise for
The Teaching Church: Congregation as Mentor

Wisdom doesn't just come down from on high—it bubbles up from below, too. Pulpit and pew share sacred space in the church, and God uses each and both to make congregations healthy and strong. Sarah Shelton and Chris Hamlin are pastors with the humility to listen to the voices of the people and share their wisdom with us. Teaching congregations are always also learning communities, as this good book shows.

—George A. Mason
Senior Pastor, Wilshire Baptist Church, Dallas, Texas
Author of *Preparing the Pastors We Need: Reclaiming the Congregation's Role in Training Clergy*

There is no question but that Chris Hamlin and Sarah Shelton are nudging churches and clergy in the right direction with *The Teaching Church: Congregation as Mentor*. As teaching churches participate with their ministers and the seminaries and schools of theology from which the ministers graduate, a new vista of collaboration is appearing. And, frankly, as we move at warp speed into the twenty-first century, 'doing church' will require the best efforts of all the people and organizations involved!

—Ron Grizzle
Director, The Center for Teaching Churches

Smyth & Helwys Publishing, Inc.
6316 Peake Road
Macon, Georgia 31210-3960
1-800-747-3016

The paper used in this publication meets the minimum requirements of
American National Standard for Information Sciences—
Permanence of Paper for Printed Library Materials.
ANSI Z39.48–1984. (alk. paper)

Library of Congress Cataloging-in-Publication Data

Hamlin, Christopher M.
The teaching church : the congregation as mentor /
by Christopher M. Hamlin and Sarah Jackson Shelton.
pages cm
Includes bibliographical references and index.
ISBN 978-1-57312-682-3 (pbk. : alk. paper)
1. Clergy--Post-ordination training. 2. Theology--Study and teaching (Continuing education)
3. Religious gatherings--Christianity. I. Shelton, Sarah Jackson. II. Title.
BV4165.H36 2013
253--dc23

2013020633

THE TEACHING CHURCH

CHURCH

CONGREGATION AS MENTOR

Also by Christopher M. Hamlin

Behind the Stained Glass: A History of Sixteenth Street Baptist Church

Also by Sarah Jackson Shelton

Sessions with Peter

This book is lovingly dedicated to our parents:

Doris Vivian Cornelius Hamlin and Herman Henry Hamlin, Sr.
and
Hermione Dannelly Jackson and James Lamar Jackson.

While they did not ever know one another, we are the direct results of their abilities to create homes in which the call of God was encouraged, nurtured, and instilled within us.

Because we are forever grateful for their dedication to us, we dedicate this book to each of them.

Contents

INTRODUCTION

By Fisher Humphreys

In order to fulfill their responsibility to prepare students for the practice of ministry, administrators and faculty members at seminaries and divinity schools engage in a continuous conversation about seminary curriculum. They add, delete, and revise academic courses. They dream up ingenious means by which seminarians can have meaningful experiences in ministry while they are still students. They require students to undertake internships, residencies, and work/study programs. They offer studies leading to the Doctor of Ministry degree.

Despite these efforts by conscientious and gifted educational institutions, ministers invariably discover in their first church that they still have a great deal to learn. The question they face is how they are to learn it. Pastors find the resources they need in a variety of places: in their own reading, in peer learning groups, and in programs of continuing education, sometimes sponsored by their seminaries and divinity schools.

In this book, Christopher Hamlin and Sarah Shelton make a special contribution to pastors' quest for further learning. They show how churches—especially the first church in which one serves as the senior pastor—become effective teachers for clergy. They explore the ways that churches instruct their pastors about social ethics, conflict management, grace, and pastoral care.

Their book inverts the usual order. It is conventional to think of pastors as teachers of their people. Hamlin and Shelton know that this is true. But they also know that pastors, especially those who are beginning their ministries, do some of their most important learning at the feet of the people in their congregations.

The authors are excellent pastors. I know this because Sarah Shelton is pastor of the congregation of which my wife and I are members, and, before Sarah became our pastor, Chris Hamlin was the interim pastor of our congregation. They can write from their own experience about how much congregations teach their pastors.

But, in preparing to write this book, they did not stop with their own experiences. They secured a grant that made it possible for them to interview seventy pastors and bishops and eleven professors of religion about how congregations become teachers of pastors. Since Chris is an African-American man and Sarah is a Caucasian woman, it is understandable that their interviewees were a diverse group of males and females. They serve in ten different denominations, which is not a trivial point, because the expectations of pastors and congregations vary from one denomination to another.

And what a treasure of wisdom they elicited from those they interviewed! As I read the rich stories their interviewees told them, I was reminded that Sarah and Chris are both splendid storytellers and preachers of the gospel of Jesus Christ, and that Jesus himself was the greatest of storytellers.

I will not spoil the book for you by retelling the interviewees' stories I found most moving or the insights I found most wise. But I will tell you that I stopped repeatedly in my reading to reflect on the wisdom and to laugh or to wipe away a tear elicited by the stories. (I will permit myself a single comment on one story: If the wisdom of the fire chief doesn't ring your bell, you should check your clapper.)

It was such a pleasure to read this book. Rarely have I found such an enjoyable book to be so helpful. I believe it will be helpful to a wide range of readers. Seminary professors who read it will be better positioned to teach their students. Church members who read it will find themselves better guided as they try to help their pastors learn the craft of pastoral work. Those who are about to begin pastoral work will be better prepared to do so by reading this book, and experienced pastors who read it will better understand the processes by which their own pastoral skills have developed.

PREFACE

It all started innocently enough. We met on a regular basis at the local coffee shop located halfway between our offices. While we did the usual boasting about how good it is to be pastors of Baptist churches, our conversations often turned to the challenges we faced and if the other had any experience or advice on which the questioning pastor might build. We met to discuss difficult personalities within our respective congregations, struggling staff ministers, suicides, baby dedications, budget proposals, building campaigns, and the like. The list seemed to grow until one of us finally said to the other, "You know, they did not teach us that in seminary!"

Now we are both astute enough to realize that our days of seminary study were replete with ivory towers and professors who could slay mighty dragons. We each possess a deep appreciation for the tools that were packed into our "kingdom kits" for the practical experiences in ministry that occur in everyday congregational life. Therefore, there is no desire to criticize the institutions of higher learning from which we each graduated. There are many aspects of parish ministry, however, for which there is no textbook. We frequently lead by trusting our instincts and, hopefully, by following the leadership of Spirit. We wondered, do other ministers feel this way? If the seminary is not the teaching institution to fill in these gaps, what institution teaches ministers how to be pastors?

In 2008 and 2009, we began to ask our peers. In fact, we interviewed fifty-six male and fourteen female pastors; thirty-seven of whom were Baptists, seven Episcopalians, eight United Methodists, seven Presbyterians, two United Church of Christ members, two Roman Catholics, and one each of Disciples, non-denominational, AMEZ, AME, and CME. Two bishops were interviewed as well as eleven professors of religion and theology (one woman and ten men).

This is a total of eighty-one interviews. The tapes of the interviews were transcribed.

After reviewing the transcriptions, we began to see a few themes emerge. This book is a presentation of those themes. They are told in the words of each interviewee. While all stories are not quoted word for word, we aimed for accuracy of each person's message as well as intent. The stories, as told in the speakers' voices, have not been softened or formalized except to add punctuation. We believe that these selections are sacred stories of experiences that come as a result of being called to serve Christ's church. For that noble calling, years of preparation have been devoted to learning from those who strive to develop men and women for ministry, but is it possible for seminary professors to teach everything that is required for leadership in Christ's church? No! Is it possible for the divinity school to provide all the necessary tools that ensure success for everyone who serves the church? No! Could it be that the church, its people, and the life events experienced within the context of the faith community become the educational experiences that mold and shape ministers into pastors? Yes!

The partnership that exists between the pastor and the people, between the academy and the community is a marvelous opportunity to witness grace at work. When men and women sincerely respond to the ancient call of proclaiming God's word, being priests among and with the people and in the community, God does bless the work and the calling. Those interviewed for this project give great witness to God's presence in their ministries and work. They cover the gamut of service to the church of Christ and God's people. They have been and remain priests in the community whose work has demonstrated a commitment to their personal families as well as their congregational families. We are grateful to the eighty-plus clergypersons who shared their stories, who sacrificed time to be interviewed, who trusted us to hold in sacredness their experiences and to treat them with dignity, respect, and confidentiality. Should you recognize your own story or that of a peer or even that of a congregation, we ask that you respect the story as sacred and do everything within your power to protect the storyteller.

The Resource Center for Pastoral Excellence at Samford University provided a grant to encourage this research, and our respective congregations and places of service—Tabernacle Baptist Church, Baptist Church of the Covenant, and the University of Alabama at Birmingham's 1917 Clinic (all of Birmingham, Alabama)—allowed us the time to interview and write. Bridget Rose served as our editor. We are deeply grateful for each one's patience and encouragement.

In addition, to our families—Sara, Kyle, Jermaine; Lloyd, David, and Dannelly—we express our abiding gratitude for your personal support in yet one more project that often meant we were not completely available to you. Thank you for your constant encouragement and the ways you remain faithful to the calling of being the pastor's family with grace.

Respectfully submitted,
Christopher M. Hamlin
Sarah Jackson Shelton

Chapter 1

The Seminary Experience

The work of theological schools is to facilitate learning for a religious vocation. Kathleen Cahalan, associate professor at Saint John's University School of Theology and Seminary, says that the seminary experience is to highlight six practices of ministry and how to think theologically about each. These practices are teaching, preaching, worship, pastoral care, administration (stewardship), and prophecy (social gospel).[1] Those interviewed for this project expressed appreciation for professors who not only knew their subject matter well but also had pastoral experience in these areas. The ability to say, "I have actually done this and it works," brought relevance to the classroom that many students respected and needed. One professor told his students, "I really believe in the classics curriculum. You don't need it in your thirties and forties, but there will come a day when you aren't going to be the charming, young person on the way up that has a bright future. You will just be our pastor, stuck out here, and then the only thing that can keep you going is theological and the only good reason to be here is christological."

Professors face a host of challenges in those who attend their institutions. When interviewed, they mentioned the idealistic student who just wants to preach Jesus. The growing majority of students has no desire to serve the local church but are looking for maverick or nontraditional settings that have an air of anti-institutionalism. They are those who want to do God's work without the first bit of study in contextual criticism or theology. Additionally, there are the conservatives and the liberals who dig in their heels so hard that there is no cultural context or personal connection with the people they are called to serve, only the propagation of their theological stances.

While professors deal with their students' predispositions in and out of the classroom, we found that the vast majority of seminary graduates looked on their seminary experience as "golden." Appreciation was expressed across the board for the tools of ministry with which they were equipped. Favorite classes ranged from pastoral care to preaching, from theology to church history. The varied favorites reflected the varied personalities and interests of each interviewee. In addition, we found that pastors could easily list classes they would most like to return to take. These clustered around the daily challenges of ministry, in particular conflict resolution and family systems theory. Because seminaries have highly specialized faculties, many of the interviewees confessed uncertainty as seminarians about the practicality of some courses. Having been in the practice of ministry, however, many would now like to retake these courses in order to find and understand a connection.

One person interviewed mentioned that he went to seminary hoping to focus his attention on church planting. The seminary offered a church growth emphasis, but it did not have anything specifically tailored to his desire to plant churches. Realizing his unique problem, he said, "I kind of had to figure out that church planting was a calling from God on my own. Nobody really taught that to me or explained that to me. The only kind of church starting that I knew about, even when I was graduating from seminary, was church splits. . . ."

Another minister, whose journey in ministry took him in a different direction, stated that the seminary he attended should emphasize the need of helping students prepare for their first church by insisting that there is a partnership between the seminary and student. He recommended that students serve in a congregation in some way while in seminary. "If you're just going to classes and don't have . . . on-the-ground experiences, I think you're going to miss or not understand fully the way that grass-roots theology operates at the church."

Another pastor commented that it would have been helpful for his seminary professors to have experience working in the church. As the pastor of a rural congregation of people who worked primarily in agriculture, he longed for some instruction from the seminary about how to deal with difficult individuals in the congregation. Instead, he received his encouragement to love those who were the most troubling from a gentleman in the church. It came after a Wednesday evening business meeting. "'Pastor, [the church member said,] the people that give you the most trouble are the people you are going to have to choose to love the most. It's easy to love those who won't back you in a corner. But those who give you the most trouble, that's who you have to love the most.' And later on in my ministry [, said the pastor,] I began to realize the reality of that and I began to put it into practice." The seminary did not teach this lesson. "No," the pastor concluded, "my seminary didn't know what was going on. I mean, those guys spend more time in the libraries than they do in the pulpit."

A pastor whose journey led him into a denominational leadership role stated that one thing that helped him most was serving in staff positions in local churches before he became a senior pastor. He served under two different styles of pastors, and what he learned from each one made this pastor long for a word from the seminary about how to balance a teaching ministry with a pastoral ministry. Rather than view them as in conflict or exclusionary, he desired a complementary path. "You know," he said, "that's what a shepherd does. He not only feeds the sheep, but he must tend the flock that he's become the overseer of."

A consistent theme among the interviewed pastors was that a lot of learning takes place within the congregation:

Interviewee: I don't think congregations realize what all they teach. I think that just the experience of living day by day and month by month and year by year within a community of people as they are going through change and as you're going through change, and life experiences are unfolding and rising that you don't see coming, and the fact that you're a person that they would welcome in or invite into the most private moments in their lives, teaches you an awful lot about trust of yourself and your own competencies that you didn't even know were in there. I don't think seminary can teach that, and I don't think seminary can teach the synthesis between the skills that they are placing into you and then prepare you for ways in which those are going to be fleshed out within an opportunity to offer ministry. I think congregations teach those things; I think congregations teach you.

Another pastor holds a similar view on congregational learning, adding that the congregation taught him about integrity.

Interviewee: The congregation has taught me who I am, what the meaning of life is, and what really matters. [. . . When] I got to seminary, [. . .] I did not speak the theological language, the seminary language, as one outside Christ's church. I didn't come to a theological school to learn theology. My relational theology came with me, and I left with it, and I think the congregation has given me my language. I think they have given me an understanding of God that [means] a whole lot. Congregations also taught me about healing [and] to allow myself to sometimes be patient, how to trust myself and welcome the trust of others, [and] to be part of the healing process in the lives of other people. I don't know if I would have learned that outside of a community of faith.

Daniel Aleshire, president of the Association of Theological Schools, says that seminaries are to provide opportunities for teaching and learning with one foot in an accredited academy and the other in the ecclesial community.[2] He says, "Theological learning is not so much for the accumulation of knowledge or the development of skills as it is for the formation of leaders in whom dispositions, knowledge and skills coinhere with integrity." And Kathleen Cahalan says that a fully integrated student-minister is one who will have "full knowledge, complete competence in all ministerial skills and a fully mature vocational identity [that] is beyond reach" in any seminary setting.[3]

This complete package may be anticipated in seminary, but it must be refined in actual ministry. Integration occurs best in the local parish when the minister is able to discern, evaluate, and judge situations in light of a community's beliefs and practices, with the aim of nurturing ever deeper and more faithful forms of Christian discipleship. To this end, ministers should seek to maintain and develop personal dispositions for continued learning and reflection on Scripture, history, and theology; they must continuously hone their preaching skills; and they should strive to strengthen personal as well as corporate faith. Our research found that achieving these goals is the challenge. New ministers faced the challenge of maintaining ongoing opportunities for learning in their first church placements.

NOTES

1. Kathleen A. Cahalan, "Introducing Ministry and Fostering Integration," *For Life Abundant: Practical Theology, Theological Education, and Christian Ministry*, ed. Dorothy Bass and Craig Dykstra (Grand Rapids MI: Eerdmans, 2008) 97.

2. Dale T. Irvin, "Precarious Institutions," *The Christian Century* 126/4 (24 February 2009): 43.

3. Cahalan, "Introducing Ministry," 113.

Chapter 2

The First Church Is Instrumental to Pastoral Identity

Seminary graduates whose goal is to become a pastor anxiously await the first interview and the first call to join the ranks of the "great cloud" of those currently serving God's church and those who have served it through the years. These men and women often have illusions of grandiose ministry and easy answers that will soon be challenged. Whatever their expectations and whatever they think they have learned, they cannot truly anticipate the shape of their ministry until they enter their first churches.

The Reverend Tim Schenck developed a guide, *From Seminary to Parish: Navigating Your First Clergy Job Search*, that offers comparative insights of the pastor search process. He wrote,

> Clergy deployment would be much easier if the Church used the Saint Matthias model of placement (Acts 1:15-26). The death of Judas led to a clear vacancy in the apostolic ministry. This position had to be filled quickly so Peter suggested a straightforward placement system. Two candidates were nominated, the disciples prayed, cast lots, and Matthias became an apostle. It was quick, easy, and the Holy Spirit was in complete control. Matthias and Joseph, known as Barsabbas, didn't have to write resumes, meet with search committees, consult with their bishops, or negotiate contracts.[1]

Unfortunately, the church does not use the methods of the Apostles in selecting pastors. The call of a pastor to his or her first church can be intimidating, scary, and emotional. Equally so, it can be a rewarding experience and a teachable moment.

Prominent pastor H. Beecher Hicks, of Metropolitan Baptist Church in Washington, D.C., included a job description for a pastor-preacher in his book, *Preaching through a Storm: Confirming the Power of Preaching in the Tempest of Church Conflict*:

> WANTED: Honest, trustworthy, positive, highly spiritual pastor to lead large inner-city church. Must be (a) consummate preacher, tireless teacher, willing to visit all sick in ten hospitals and fifteen nursing homes by noon on Tuesdays. Limited support staff. Must attend prayer meetings, preside over boards, supervise all personnel. Must be politically astute to deal with church infrastructure. Must be emotionally well adjusted, spend sufficient time with family, willing to work sixteen hours per day. Organizing, administration, and fundraising skills required. Will not be involved in money management. Candidates will be required to maintain academic currency with theological thought and be actively involved in community affairs. Must not be too liberal, too conservative, or given to extensive evangelism. Moderate salary designed to ensure continuous humility. Must be well dressed, but not flashy. Must be independent, adventuresome, able to initiate and respond creatively to all situations. Must be fearless, flawless, and willing to take all risks. Sermons limited to twenty minutes, most volume. Subjects must be consistently brilliant, creative, funny, noncontroversial. Applicants must apply in person and in public. Excellent opportunity for self-starter.[2]

The above description would likely overwhelm a seminarian close to graduation and beginning a search for their first placement, yet it highlights the many responsibilities and expectations, which are often not verbalized, of most pastors and the roles that most pastors attempt to fulfill.

Much like the medical student who completes his or her coursework and then enters into an internship or residency program for a complete immersion into the everyday life of a physician, the seminarian takes a first church. The fondness with which these churches are discussed, the reverence that seems to characterize the reminiscing, and the gratitude expressed for these first churches speaks to the education that continues in, through, and between a congregation and its pastor. First churches seem to be the graduate school of theological learning. A common statement from the pastors interviewed was that first churches gave them opportunities to put theory into practice. The response of the people shaped how the minister developed an identity that lasted throughout his or her career. It determined how they would approach congregants and how they practiced their trade for their entire lives. One said, "In the three years that I spent at my first church, I learned more about loving people than [in] all my years put together. I started getting a handle on the expectations of the people. The needs of the people . . . and the needs of the community . . . should drive a minister's ministry."

As a seminary student, one pastor was fortunate to have a student appointment in a small church. Because he had to balance studies, family, and his congregation of approximately 100 people, what he learned in seminary had to be quickly applied to congregational life. "The whole seminary curriculum thing was transformed," he said, "and I saw real connections with real people's lives. I decided that, hopefully, I could help people in their lives. I went to seminary not planning to be a pastor, but I did [become a pastor]." Reflecting on this experience, he concluded that his first appointment was to a healthy congregation. Even the two or three "cranky" members were insulated and not damaging to the health of the congregation.

Another senior pastor talked about the church teaching him to be patient: "We need to have patience, and we need to deal with individuals where they are. They all come to us, first of all, in different ways, and they're at all different levels on a different journey. There's not a brush that you can paint the entire congregation with; you have to meet people where they are and deal with them compassionately."

One interviewee also described his first pastorate in a 100-member church. Because of its small size, he was concerned that it might be a congregation that was suspicious of those with higher degrees in education. So when he walked in the door, the first question posed seemed to support his wariness. "Do you have a robe?" they asked. Not sure if this would be a deal breaker or not, he hesitated to answer. Then the person said that they simply wanted to know because, if their ministers did not have a robe, they always bought them one!

Another pastor, meanwhile, tells of accepting his first church in a prominent historic church in a large urban community. He shared the story of being asked not to preach in a robe. The chairman of the board of deacons, the de facto leader of the congregation in the absence of a pastor, informed him that a robe was not necessary. The new pastor was aware of the former pastors and knew that they always wore robes while preaching. In a later discussion, the new pastor discovered that the chairman was making an attempt to change the "flavor" of the worship service and the perception that the church was a stiff, overly intelligent congregation.

A judicatory leader spoke of being in his first parish and the valuable lessons he learned: "My first parish in [a community] taught me lessons that no seminary could; it would be illegal for seminaries to try to teach me some of that stuff! I think they taught me— particularly rural churches with people who had been denied access to the educational system—that they are still intellectual in some deep ways. And this was one of my jolts coming from [a prestigious divinity school]."

A pastor shared his similar experience of being in his first church that was rural. He said, "We [our congregation] were like a family. And when I went back to graduate school after being there as the pastor for eight years, what I missed most intensely was that web of wonderful, rich, deep relationships which we had in the church; that's what I missed tremendously for years."

Perhaps it is because most recent seminary graduates have some awareness of their inexperience and their confidence is low, or maybe they have not had too many gray-haired ladies tell them how wonderful they are (yet), or maybe seminary humbled them just enough that they are willing to continue their education in and among the people who make up their first congregation. Interestingly, first churches also seem to be made up of people who are willing to say to a fresh, young pastor, "Here, let me show you how to be effective."

They also seem to be exceptionally tolerant of mistakes, initial sermons, and disorganization. And in spite of it all, they remain open to helping the pastor find his or her voice and to teach a few lessons of pastoral care and finesse along the way. Consider the following example:

Interviewee: When I served at my first church, a gruesome murder occurred one summer [in our community]. The victim was a mentally [challenged] teenager in our congregation. When the policeman came by the parsonage to tell me that they had found her dead body, he asked me to come to the police station to meet the girl's parents and talk to them. When he left, I froze. I had never been close to any crisis like that, and I didn't know what to do or say. Cancer? No problem. Heart attack? Easy. Even suicide. I had become a pro at responding to the survivors, but a rape-murder of a mentally challenged teenage girl? I was a lost ball in high weeds. So God sent me the fire chief in town. His wife was our organist, but he himself was a Methodist. I didn't care what he was when he called me before I left and asked me if I wanted him to go with me. I whispered, "Yes." He suggested that we first stop by the girl's grandmother's home to tell her. When we pulled up in front, she was sitting on the front porch rocking. As soon as she saw the fire chief get out of his truck, she started screaming, "I know why you're here. Tell me she's not dead!" Again, I froze. I whispered, "What do I do?" He quietly said, "You've never done this before have you? Just watch me, I'll show you what to do." And he did. He walked right up to where she was sitting, bent down on one knee, took her hands in his, and said, "I'm so sorry, but they've found her body. And she's dead." And as she cried and cried, he didn't say anything. He just knelt there and held her hand and patted her shoulders. When we got to the police station, he repeated the same pattern with the immediate family and again showed me how to respond in the worst of times—through incarnational grace and presence. Years later, I got a better understanding of what all happened that afternoon when a conference leader commented, "At your first church, you don't know how to pastor. So the people have to teach you."

One pastor referenced not being prepared to preach when he graduated from seminary. He stated that could have been his fault or that of the professor, whom he didn't like much. He felt inadequately prepared, but his skills were polished through congregational experience.

One pastor expressed much joy in sharing a moment of profound meaning and learning. The experience taught him that the church does not ordain clergy. The people do.

Interviewee: It all started with me really right out of seminary. I was not ordained a priest yet. I was still a deacon and actually it was [nice]. Someone brought some African-American children to our church from [a community program based at the church]. And those children were playing in the church and I was telling them they couldn't be running around. And so I said, "Y'all come back on Sunday; we'd love to see you." They came back on that Sunday and one of the [youth workers] brought these children up to the altar. It's typical for clergy to bless children who aren't baptized. So, I was a deacon serving, but I wanted to make that trip to the altar special because they had come to [our church] and we had taken care of them. It was a mighty powerful moment for the children. I went ahead and blessed the children with the cross and afterwards the children were [curious]. And so the lady that was with me explained to them that this was a cross . . . . Couple days later I'm in my office talking to my boss and these kids, 5 years and 6 years old, they said, "Excuse me, we are here to see the preacher." And [my boss] said, "Yes." And the kid pointed at me and said, "Chili needs one of those crosses." He brought a kid off the streets for me to bless him. And see, I'm still a deacon. And I realized that Chili had ordained me. . . . That's when I realized I had been ordained.

The first church experience becomes foundational for all future ministry assignments. If the pastor learns from the seminary and transfers the sum of his or her learning to the congregation as the congregation learns from the pastor, the mold is set for a positive experience for all three. A retired pastor with forty-three years of service stated that the pastor doesn't have all the answers. "Rather, he [or she] struggles with the congregation to address the complex concerns of persons, families, community and world. It involves learning to deal with diversity and conflict."

The first church experience plays a vital role in equipping the pastor with tools for his or her ongoing development and ensuring that congregations will continue to grow and serve not only the congregants but also the community. A viable partnership that exists between the pastor and church is a sign of the usefulness of the congregation in the ongoing training of the pastor.

NOTES

1. Tim Schenck, *From Seminary to Parish: Navigating Your First Clergy Job Search*, self-published, 2001, p. 6; online at http://archive.episcopalchurch.org/documents/From_Seminary_to_Parish.pdf.

2. H. Beecher Hicks, *Preaching through a Storm: Confirming the Power of Preaching in the Tempest of Church Conflict* (Grand Rapids MI: Ministry Resources Library, 1987) 157.

Chapter 3

The Congregation Teaches Social Ethics

While seminaries often warn students that their congregations may be slow to embrace change or to move in more "advanced" theological directions, the majority of the ministers interviewed referred to their congregations as avid students who embraced opportunities to learn and grow. This is particularly true in the area of social ethics or in the arena where church members move and live. One pastor commented on seminaries not painting the full potential of congregations: "I have found that congregations are far more open to accepting change and embracing new ideas and taking new approaches than the seminary led me to believe they would be."

Another pastor shared the story of being led to rethink his conservative teaching and how his congregation followed his leadership:

Interviewee: I think my congregation taught me the importance of empowering people in the church to do ministry and not to depend on professional staff. I was reared in a conservative denomination that is very big in [my state] and so I was raised biblically that women could not be pastors. That was liberal, unbiblical—you know all that, and I had that view even when I went to [seminary] and when I started my first church and my second church. I maintained that understanding, and that is what I taught. But while I was pastoring in Massachusetts, I worked on my DMin degree. That is when I really began to seek from Scriptures my theological and biblical basis for [controversial] subjects like slavery, Sabbath, war, and women and those type things. I realized that I was wrong and so I went back to my church in Massachusetts . . . and got in the pulpit and apologized to them because I had said [things] to them from the pulpit that were not correct biblically or theologically, and that I was sorry. I encouraged them to stick with me, and we would try to go back and relearn this together. To my surprise, it wasn't as big of an issue for them as it was for me. They were ready to embrace it much sooner than I was.

A moment of poignant reality came for another pastor as he was preaching:

Interviewee: In the early part of my ministry, I had an old gentleman in one of those rural churches. This one was a short fellow, in his seventies. He would stand up in the middle of the sermon and say, 'You have to tell the whole truth. You have to shell the corn good. You have to tell it all.' I mean right in the middle of the sermon. And I'd say, 'Brother, I'm trying to!' And what he was saying was don't give us any false hope here. Give us reality, if you can. And I didn't know that I could.

Today's denominations and local congregations are wrestling with many issues from same-sex unions to poverty; from political involvement to the environment; from women in ministry to welcoming diversity, and the list continues. A retired pastor shared what happened to his congregation that forever changed parishioners' perspective on a controversial issue.

Interviewee: When we had a group of gays that came in [to the church], everybody was scared. We lost our biggest givers—two doctors—and we didn't have any money. I started telling these gay folks, I said, "Listen, if this is going to work, you're going to have to show this congregation that you are just like them and no different. If you can do that, we may win this battle. But it's left up to you to do that." Bless their hearts, we had this [anniversary] party the other night, these two gay guys who had been together for twenty-five years, they were shackin' up since they can't get married. I bet sixty percent of the people at that party were straight and members of this church were celebrating this occasion and it was just wonderful.

A pastor does not have to be in a congregation long before it becomes apparent that each person lives within a cultural context that affects who they are. While some crises are easily identified (such as the 9/11 national crisis, a natural disaster, or a community tragedy), many of the congregants' cultural context challenges are private. They often deal with heavy burdens in isolation. With time and the development of trust, the pastor will become aware of these. While congregants' fears may remain private, some event in the community of faith may trigger a powerful yet often unexplained response. For instance, after hearing a sermon stating the reasons why the priest of a parish could not support the ordination of gays and lesbians, a church member began a new public routine. After receiving Communion each week, he would walk from the altar to the columbarium (a mausoleum-type structure where the ashes of deceased persons are kept, memorialized and entombed), which was also in the front of the sanctuary, and place a kiss on the niche that held his son's ashes. His son, a homosexual, had committed suicide due to the lack of acceptance in his community. The father's action was a quiet rebellion against the priest's sermon and presented a challenge to the faith community of their responsibility to love, receive, and celebrate the gifts of all people.

A female minister told of a time when she preached an Advent sermon and referenced her own experience of being pregnant. A woman in the church was furious about the sermon. Only later did the pastor discover that the angry woman's daughter had had an abortion. The minister reflected, "I didn't do anything wrong, but she had a lot of her own stuff. . . . Sometimes people don't intend to, but they are sitting out there with a lot of different experiences" that they act out on the pastor.

Another female pastor commented on the challenges of being a woman in ministry and being surprised that her opposition did not come from men. "I think . . . I've had more trouble with women . . . than I've had with men," she said. "And the one man that I had trouble with in [a particular community] was being led by a woman to cause the trouble."

While some interviewees were uncomfortable, others spoke openly about issues of social ethics found within their congregations. Such issues included the mentally challenged, homosexuality, constitution reform, divorce, women's rights, domestic violence, foster care for children, and racial equality. One said that he was surprised to find that his congregation "wanted to be engaged in justice issues if they had the right kind of leadership. I think I had assumed in the past that they just maybe weren't that interested, but they are. They are deeply moved when I share with them some of the injustices."

One pastor talked about social ethics as the field in which she "chooses her battles." Because she has thoughtfully connected issues with Scripture in the past, she feels that the congregation will follow her leadership into other areas, but not until it becomes an issue in her mind. "My congregation knows that I'm not afraid to approach the subject," she said, "but that I will only approach it when there is a need. I would address it with integrity and not in a way that would be hurtful or harmful to anybody."

Yet another pastor had this to say:

Interviewee: Most of the social ministries that I've been involved with came to me through members of the congregation. They told me "here is what I know about poverty and hunger, death and AIDS; let me tell you about it." In other words, it has come to me from the people on the front lines, not out of the blue. And they've often brought me the things that I've needed to know in order to respond and understand. The clergy having difficulties and who stand apart, are those who cannot relate and cannot learn.

One pastor faced a challenging ethical situation with a congregation and handled it without direct conflict. This newly appointed pastor came into a highly diverse congregation. The openness of the membership allowed for flexibility and creativity in ministry, so the pastor was surprised to find active anxiety regarding a family in the congregation who was expecting their first child. Wisely, the pastor took some church leaders aside to inquire about the concern that seemed inconsistent with the church's convictions. In that conversation, it was divulged that while the church had children in every imaginable family configuration, this was the first time that the congregation had witnessed a pregnancy from its beginning to its ending in a family that had two mothers. For the full nine months, the pastor listened as members expressed concern over how to handle the baby dedication.

After a particularly difficult conversation with some church members one night, the pastor was talking about it on the car ride home. The teenage son, also in the car, said, "Aren't you missing the point? Isn't the child the focus of a baby dedication and not what church members think or who the parents are?" And at that moment the pastor's perspective began to change.

On Christmas Eve, the congregation gathered in the dimly lit sanctuary with their extended family members. The air was full of Christmas excitement, hope, and joy. Only when they looked at the bulletin did they see that the pastor had decided to include the baby dedication of the newest addition in this special family service. Upon entering the sanctuary, the pastor noted that the mothers were sitting on the front pew. A few family members sat on the pew behind, and the baby was bundled in blankets with a lace cap on its head. The charter members, however, were seated on the last pew in the sanctuary.

The time in the service arrived for the baby dedication. Silence descended as the pastor stepped down to receive the baby and then returned to the pulpit. Knowing that the congregation was unsettled, the pastor only talked to the baby. There were no promises sought from the congregation. There was no standing of the parents before the congregation. The pastor simply told the baby all that was hoped and prayed for whenever a gift from God is given. Then, almost as if on cue, the baby closed its eyes and went to sleep. So this wet-behind-the-ears pastor did a wise thing. This pastor preached while holding that baby. During the entire sermon, the baby slept while the pastor cradled it and talked about another baby who was born in circumstances that the world had difficulty accepting.

As the pastor finished the sermon and brought the baby back to the parents so that Communion could be served, a remarkable thing happened. From the back row of the sanctuary, the "mother" of the church—the one who holds everything and everyone together, who nurses the sick and holds the hands of the hurting, who blesses the brides and organizes the meals for the bereaved—got up, walked down the aisle, and asked if she could hold the baby so that the parents could receive Communion together. And when she scooped that little bundle up in her arms, she sat on the front row so that everyone who received Communion had to walk by her and the baby. As the service progressed, you could feel the need to control, the fear, and the anxiety fall away. In her receiving of that child, the congregation and the pastor accepted the baby and the baby's parents as every misgiving that they had carried for months fell away.

Even the most seasoned pastor takes a huge risk to address issues of social ethics, because the congregation will respond in a variety of ways to the prophetic voice in the pulpit. Scripture, such as Jesus' embracing children against the wishes of adults (Matt 19.13ff) or Jesus' ignoring societal norms by talking with a Samaritan woman (John 4.4ff), gives testimony to this dynamic. While appreciation may result from concrete actions of justice, there is also sometimes a backlash of criticism from which the pastor may never recover. This is when the congregation begins to teach difficult lessons. A retired pastor stated that in situations like this, "[Some congregations teach] the pastor that 'church' isn't about promoting and maintaining an institution—rather, it's about growing as an inclusive community being shaped by the Spirit of Jesus, a community engaged in the work of compassion, justice, and peace in the world."

Yet there are moments when the pastor, taking a tremendous stand for a social justice issue, faces the cruel reality that people may not be in the same place of understanding as the pastor in thought or practice. One pastor shared how he tried to incorporate a deaf ministry in his church to meet the needs of nine deaf people in the geographical area surrounding the church. He poignantly and passionately shared a profound moment of tension and embarrassment.

Interviewee: I met with the deacons and I told them I'd like to start this ministry. And they said, they knew it was a personal thing with me, but it was a principle thing with the other deaf people. So they brought it up to the church on Wednesday night. We had [members] to stand up and say, "All he wants to do is get [derogatory word used to describe African Americans] in this church." And I'll never forget—my son, my son who is the lawyer now but was seventeen years of age then—on our way home that night he said, "Daddy, let's leave this church." But I said, "No, we aren't going to leave." So I started the deaf ministry and [a school].

This pastor continued to share the story of an African-American gynecologist whose office was nearby and whose patients included several members of his church. This physician and her sister, whose father was a minister, wanted to worship there because it would be convenient for her schedule. The pastor invited them to come.

Interviewee: And so, they came. I caught enough hell about that. The deacons wanted to meet with me. I said, "Her office is right across the street. As a matter of fact, two or three of the ladies in this church are patients of hers. When she makes her calls on Sunday mornings she can't get to her church, and she'd like to come here. And I see no problem with that." And so, they said, "Well we need to meet with them." And I said, "Well if you are going to meet with them, you will meet with me and the staff."

The deacons first stated that they had nothing against their race and suggested that the physician and her sister worship in their own church, meaning in an all-black church. The embarrassed pastor apologized to the women. He talked about all those present bleeding the same red blood. He told them, "The problem is my skin is white and your skin is dark and they [the deacons and members] can't accept that. And I'm sorry we've put you through this."

Not long after that incident, other issues arose that led the pastor to resign. More than five hundred people were in Sunday school at the time of his resignation. A year later, attendance had dropped to under three hundred. Today, the average attendance is fifty to sixty in Sunday school.

Several other pastors spoke of knowing how deeply their congregations experienced all levels of pain and yet worked to conceal it. "I have discovered that people will go to great lengths to keep their pain and suffering private," one pastor said. "Our congregation, while not exempt from social issues, does not talk about problems openly, even in a private setting. This causes me to listen and be extremely sensitive to the membership as I attempt to understand the things they say and don't say," he concluded.

Issues of social justice, of course, extend beyond local congregations. A judicatory leader spoke clearly regarding the role of the church to address issues that not only affect the church but also the global community:

Interviewee: Certainly the whole question of poverty, hunger, and economic injustice seems to come up constantly. In a society where so few have a lot and so many have a little, there's constant struggle with how the church can address poverty and economic issues and build a bridge between the needs of the world and the people of the church so that the people of the church can actually be involved. I think that in [our state] the issue is tax reform. Tax reform is the single biggest issue which has direct impact on economic justice issues and schools and human needs. [That's] where the church needs to be active and social.

These stories relating to ethics and issues of social justice reflect the struggles of many congregations and pastors. Some issues that result in church conflict have been mentioned here, and others are addressed in chapter 4. As well, these kinds of issues often result in a community of faith reflecting moments when God's grace is evident. Some of these stories are related in chapter 5.

As the church confronts social issues, it finds itself seeking effective ways of managing conflict. In the chapter to follow, some pastors speak forthrightly about various challenges that tested their abilities to resolve multiple issues.

Chapter 4

The Congregation Teaches Conflict Management

"There is cruelty in the church. It can be about the cruelest place in the world." (—an interviewee)

Henri Nouwen states, "A Christian community is therefore a healing community not because wounds are cured and pains are alleviated, but because wounds and pains become openings or occasions for a new vision." He further states that, "Mutual confession then becomes a mutual deepening of hope, and sharing weakness becomes a reminder to one and all of the coming strength."[1]

Our hope is that in the confessions that follow in this chapter, some healing has taken place and a new vision of mutuality between pastor and congregations may occur. Some of the stories we've retold; others are told in the voices of the interviewees.

STORIES OF CONFLICT WITH CHURCH MEMBERS

"I'm going to ruin this church."

Interviewee: The most memorable incident [regarding conflict in the church] is related to our associate pastor. He got into a running conflict with a member of the church. It escalated to the point where one day the two of them were in the hall outside his office, and this woman [created an atmosphere of conflict], and so he said, "Let's just finish this. Let's just go ahead and have this out right now." They went into his office, and basically every insult she aimed at him, he said back to her. If she said, "You're an idiot." He said, "You're an idiot."

Finally, she got so angry that she just left. It precipitated her leaving the church. The immediate reaction was that the associate pastor was a hero for getting rid of her because she intimidated people. She was angry. There had been conflict before I got there, and she had said, "I'm not leaving this church. I'm going to ruin this church." She was a bitter, angry woman, so lots of people were just relieved when she was gone, but it didn't take long after that for people to start second guessing my associate and saying, "You could've handled this a different way." It really went to the end of his time there. It was the factor that tipped the scale for him. He stayed for about a year after that, but for six months, we knew he was going to be gone. That's probably the most memorable event because it was painful for me. I just loved this guy. He was a great colleague. He might not have been the right guy for that place; I trust that. But I miss him.

Interviewer: Where is he now?

Interviewee: He's unemployed.

False Accusations

One pastor told of his decision to preach about what it had been like to grow up with his father; this was soon after the pastor returned from his father's funeral. The father, also a minister, had been a functional alcoholic. Late in life he had divorced his wife in order to be with a much younger woman with whom he had had an affair for many years. His son (the pastor we interviewed) shared about his father one Sunday in worship shortly after returning from his father's funeral. Unsure if his sermon was misunderstood or if the congregation's historical pattern of caring for its pastors became the overriding factor, the pastor was caught off guard when he found a contingency of the church leadership, along with denominational representation, waiting for him in his office. They accused him of being drunk at weddings and other church events. They even went so far as to say that the glass of water on the pulpit was alcohol in order to "brace" this pastor for worship leadership. While he insisted that the accusations were false, he agreed to receive treatment from a local in-house rehab center. The intake nurse refused his admission into the program, saying he did not meet the qualifications. When the ruse was over, the only option this minister had was to return to the routine of parish life with a congregation that had accused him falsely.

Going to Court

One pastor shared being called to a historic church. While he was drawn to the prestige of the place, he arrived only to discover that the church was in a difficult position. The congregation did not have a mechanism in place for terminating pastors, and so, in two instances, the court system had been enlisted to mediate differences between former pastors and the congregation. The public disagreements led many members to walk away. News articles in local papers made the public aware of every detail. In many cases, the church—in spite of its historical presence—became the laughing stock of the larger community.

The new pastor arrived. He was not only new to the city and the church—this was also his first full-time pastorate. The membership had dwindled to approximately one hundred active members. The average age was approximately fifty-five. The church had few young people. Ministries/church programs were barely hanging on. In addition, there was a great need for major renovations in order to preserve the historic building.

After two years and some modest growth, the congregation made the commitment to begin a capital campaign. To kick off the campaign, the congregation pledged and raised a significant amount of money. These sacrificial gifts were a strong sign of their commitment and genuine love for the church. With the renovations completed and the calling of the first full-time professional ministerial staff person, there was renewed interest in the ongoing ministry of the church. A growth trend developed for the next seven years. At the end of the eighth year, the size of the congregation had reached more than five hundred members. The community also became involved as the pastor and other church leaders began to solicit and receive funding from various community sources.

In the midst of this success, however, the church soon faced an overwhelming challenge in a lay leader. This person challenged the pastor's leadership and vision for the church, the work of the finance committee, and the ongoing success of the capital campaign. Most suggestions made by the pastor for the continued growth of the church were called into question. Unfortunately, other leaders of the church could not create a strong response to this person's allegations, and so the congregation accepted the recommendations made by this dissonant personality as being in the best interest of the church.

The relationship between the pastor and this person became combative. The pastor evaluated not only his tenure at the church but also his calling to the pastorate. Even though his ten years of effective leadership had resulted in successful growth, a completely renovated sanctuary with a restored pipe organ, and renewed positive public image, he made the hard decision to resign. Unfortunately, there was no committee to appeal to, no staff committee, no personnel committee, and no judicatory or denominational authority that could have assisted the pastor and/or the congregation at this critical juncture. The pastor was stunned that after reading his resignation, incredibly, not one person within the congregation came to his defense publicly. A group in the church had told him that they "had his back." But when he resigned, no one came forth to say that the resignation would not be received or was even untimely. No one suggested that there were better alternatives. No one made a defense, and no one expressed concern about his future well-being or that of his family. The congregation seemed content with his decision to resign without another place of service.

To add insult to injury, after the resignation, the pastor was subpoenaed to appear in court. He was to be deposed regarding accusations that he had misappropriated grant monies. The church had never received the grant in question, and, after good legal counsel, a competent judge dismissed the issue. It was revealed in the legal process that the accusations against the pastor had been made by the same person who had created unrest within the congregation. The church, however, resorted to old patterns by using the court system to deal publicly with internal and private matters. This was another black eye for the church.

While the congregation continued to be stressed, the pastor did too. It is not uncommon for pastors who experience challenges within their congregations to experience stress in their personal relationships as well. Although this pastor confessed to being in a marriage that had endured challenges prior to coming to the historic church, the experiences in that church did not support the health of his marriage. In addition, resources were not made available, and no help was sought to sustain the relationship. Stress also resulted in health-related issues. During his tenure, the pastor gradually experienced high blood pressure, heart murmurs (unusual palpitations), and high cholesterol. Eventually, his marriage ended in divorce. He became embittered against the church and desired not to pastor again. His hiatus from ministry took him to a position within an academic institution of higher learning.

When Is Enough Enough?

Interviewee: Congregations have said "no" to me. For instance, about the budget assessment [an annual collection made in some denominations by their governing hierarchy]: I told them what the budget [amount] is—a number given by the denomination's presiding elder—and the congregation said that's too much. I told them we don't have the authority to change it because we don't have the authority to change the amount that was given to us. And so they didn't pay it. The presiding elder thought it was my responsibility to pay the difference. My take on that is "no." I had foregone salary and I had contributed enough. But no, I'm not going to borrow money to pay an assessment. The presiding elder said I should be removed from that charge because I refused to pay the assessment and my response was, "Okay, move me. It's okay." The congregation said "no" again to paying the assessment. So there was nothing I could do. I don't think they were saying "no" because they were deliberately being mean. I think it was because [the congregation] was a small number. [. . . They were being over-taxed.] And they knew that I had given salary toward it and that my family had paid. We had given

money, our tithes and sacrificial offerings. They had reached their
limit, and I had reached my limit financially in terms of what I could
afford to pay. So, it is frightening that when the congregation says
'no,' . . . They say "no" about a lot of things.

"I was on the verge of hating her."

Interviewee: The previous pastor had warned me about a woman
who was prone to call the preacher out from the congregation [i.e.,
would make bold and loud comments during the sermon]. So when
she called me out, my wife knew I was about to jump over the rail
and meet her outside and let her know.

Interviewer: So what did you do that morning?

Interviewee: I sat there. I told the folks, "It's time to pray." I started
praying. She started slamming the door. The folks got up and they
started praying. I told the folks we were not fighting against flesh and
blood. It was spiritual warfare. It was hard. It was difficult. When she
got sick, I went to see her. I told her she needed communion in her
heart, because I couldn't let the evil overtake her. It taught me, but
I'm still learning. . . . It was hard work, every day.

In the situation above, the pastor had difficulty controlling his emotions and his words in a situation where he felt personally attacked.
The pastor said that he was determined and had asked the Lord to
teach him how to love because he really disliked the woman. He continued, "I was on the verge of hating her. I would be in that pulpit
and I would feel the evil. I would have headaches. It was a difficult
time, but it taught me some things. Part of what it taught me was
how to love."

Women in the Pastorate

The story of women moving more into pastoral positions reveal that
many congregations continue to discriminate and have difficulty
accepting women as senior pastors.

Interviewee: Less than twelve months before my arrival, a woman and her husband had become new Christians and joined the church. She had immediately been made chair of the Pastor-Parish Relations Committee, and her husband was elected to be Chair of the Trustees. These were the two most powerful committees in the church. He [did not work outside the home] because of a disability with an injury, and she was a traveling nurse and excellent at what she did. So when she was approached about receiving a woman as the pastor, she was thrilled at the prospect but had no idea that no one else in the church was thrilled with the idea of a woman pastor. So once I arrived, I realized that only one person wanted me there. When I moved there, the pastor before me who was on loan from another conference left all the files in the office and on top of them a magazine article about why women should not be allowed in the pulpit.

. . . . Oftentimes I would be next door at the parsonage and look out and see cars in the parking lot and discover later that all the churches [in the area] decided to do something social together but had not invited me or included me. That was really hard, and it was difficult because in the time I was there, I brought in lots of new members to that church. We did a lot of work on the facility. We did a lot of good things, and yet there were people who stayed out of church because there was a woman [pastor].

There was one homebound member whom I think may have been behind it. When I would go to visit her, I'd knock on the door and say it was the preacher, and she'd say, "Oh no. It's the preacher's wife." And I said, "No, it's the preacher, not the preacher's wife."

After the first year, they had several meetings with the district superintendent (D.S.), and they were sure they were going to get me to move. The D.S. finally said there was nobody willing to move to my church, so I would be staying. We were half-packed, but I had to stay there for another year before they moved me. I got really tired.

One of the people who most clearly didn't want me there had a mother in the nursing home. The mother remained in a fetal position and had been that way for some time. I went to see her regularly even though she never responded to anything. But one time, I went to visit and I reached over and took her hand and had prayer. At the end, just as clear as a bell, she said, "Amen." I told that story at the funeral, and the people were just staring because nobody believed that I had ever visited her. They didn't know me well enough to know that that was important to me or that I would do that or that something like that would have happened to me. It was right before I moved, and I already wanted to move, but it transformed some of their understanding as to who I was. I learned that whether people like me or want me or not, I can still do the work of God.

Dealing with Different Agendas

Interviewee: Everyone comes with some agenda attached to their lives. Some are standard barriers and some are carrying torches. I think what you learn from them is that if you're going to be their pastor and relate to them, you have to deal with their agendas and be open to their agendas. You may not embrace or support all of them, but you have to hear them. Some will not fit your faith orientation, and you're going to still have to deal with them. So you learn you have to listen to them. You also learn that you can agree to disagree. That's where I have often been with a lot of people and their agendas. It doesn't mean we can't be related to one another or share in ministry together. It doesn't mean they're wrong and you're right, even though they are often times wrong.

STORIES OF CONFLICT WITH CHURCH HIERARCHIES

For those pastors in denominations where an hierarchal form of leadership is in place, often the pastor and the congregation are at the whims of the bishop, district superintendent, presiding elder, or other authority-type leaders. Several stories clearly indicate that congregational conflict may be caused by decisions made by denominational leadership. Pastors often become the target of criticism and venomous statements from members for decisions made not by them, but by denominational leaders. Judicatory leadership wields a lot of power and influence over ministers, their families, and congregations. They can be supportive, but they can also be influenced by a congregation's desire. The fate of the clergy often rests in the hands of their bishops and district superintendents.

Going Back

A pastor had begun a multi-million [dollar] campaign at his church and was just beginning to see the positive growth for which he had hoped. The bishop, however, felt that it was time to move this pastor after only two years.

Interviewee: So I did my seven years of drought [in the new church; he was placed in a church of the bishop's choosing, not his own]. Then the bishop called to say it was time to go back to the original church because the leadership needed me. I found that the church had become divided and that the [current] pastor was inexperienced [especially with capital campaigns]. We walked into the beautiful facility, and were greeted with, "I hate you." "I just can't stand you." "I know it's not your fault, but I hate you." While some left, thirty-five joined immediately upon hearing that I was being reinstated as the new pastor.

Moving

It was proposed to a staff minister that he and his family were being moved to serve as a senior pastor at a wonderful congregation in a small, rural community. This minister had two young children, one biological child and one adopted, biracial child. The minister and his wife were concerned about the acceptance of their adopted child in such a small community. The minister's uneasiness about the placement was legitimate, so he registered his concern with judicatory leadership. The reply came in the form of an ultimatum. The minister was given a specific amount of time to report to the congregation as senior pastor.

While desiring to work in parish ministry and praying about the prospective placement, the minister was invited to consider a job that would take him out of parish ministry but keep him serving in ministry in an executive position for a non-profit. Feeling that he had no other option, he took the non-profit position and turned down the senior pastor position. Fortunately, the new position is rewarding, fits his skill set, and is affirming for his family.

However, because he left the parish ministry, the judicatory leadership continued to make life difficult for him. He found relief and acceptance for the decisions he made when new leadership came to the district and assisted in affirming an ongoing relationship with his denomination.

Throughout discussions being held with the judicatory leadership, this minister kept reminding himself, "Remember why you are doing what you are doing. People are the most important thing." Today, he serves a unique population. His "congregation" is larger than he has ever had, and the work is truly beneficial—and it is all being done in an environment of nurturing care.

Staying

One interviewee disclosed that she had been appointed to ten different churches after completing seminary. Her husband was also a pastor and often they worked in churches that were as far apart as an hour and a half. At each church, she said, she stayed for only two years with the exception of three churches where she was allowed to stay for four years each.

Interviewer: The denominational system has just moved you from place to place?

Interviewee: You agree when you're ordained to go where you are sent, and you move if you or your congregation feels that God is urging you in that direction. Theoretically, that's how moves happen. Occasionally, they will say to you, "We're going to move you. We know you don't want to move, and we know your church doesn't [want you to move], but we need you in this particular situation."

Interviewer: Does this support the theory that even in your denomination that clergy women are difficult to appoint, so they put you in rural small towns?

Interviewee: Yes. Most of my appointments have been based on whether the church has either had a woman before or is willing to take a woman. Even though it's in the book of discipline that you're not to ask, the district superintendent usually asks, before the appointment is made, if the church will accept a woman.

This pastor continued to talk about various appointments and then described this:

Interviewee: . . . After the first year, the church had several meetings with the district superintendent. The church was sure they were going to get me to move. He came back [for a second meeting], and all the people who wanted me to stay attended this meeting. He decided I was going to stay, but two weeks before the annual conference, [those who wanted me to leave] called the bishop. The district superintendent called me to say that the bishop would be calling a meeting of the cabinet. The superintendent essentially said, "They are going to fire you; pack your stuff. They're being really ugly about this, and you don't need to be put through all of that. We will meet on [the day], and I will call you when it is over." So there I was, waiting. He didn't call me. When I finally called him, he said there was no one willing to move, and I would be staying. I had to stay for another year.

ALLEVIATING THE TENSION OF CONFLICT

Henri Nouwen's work *The Wounded Healer* suggests that ministers are called to radiate hope, especially in the midst of conflict. If Nouwen is correct, the hope radiated from the minister is a signal that healing is not only possible, but desirable and the congregation is strengthened through the process. The stories captured through the interview process reveal the struggle that many pastors face as they wrestle with managing conflict.

As we began this study, we braced ourselves to hear many horror tales, and we did. But there was also a pervasive appreciation for congregations as they attempt to live their understanding of the gospel in a particular time frame and historical context. The invitation to a pastor to join his or her members in specific life situations still carries a mysterious respect. Maybe our respondents were not completely honest and wanted to appear noble. Maybe having lived through the hard time and survived, these ministers had learned valuable lessons, making them appear wiser. There were, however, enough indicators of "war wounds" to prove that the congregation is the teacher of conflict management.

Ministers can also be instrumental in managing conflict by creating environments where shared experiences can give them hope and where they can be agents of the healing process for their congregations. Ministers and congregations should not be made to believe that they are called to suffer in silence. Congregations learn to get through painful times, and the result is often a healthier ministry. Through shared experiences, they teach their pastors and ministers how to endure and persevere.

Poor communication between pastor and congregations seems to be the most prevalent cause of conflict and misunderstanding. One co-pastor said, "No one said anything to us and it [an accusation of being unconventional and unorthodox] just came out of nowhere. The thing that still makes me angry about it is that they [the congregation] still don't understand why [making unfounded accusations is] inappropriate."

One pastor, in referring to a therapy session, said that his therapist taught him that if you wish to remain at your church, you must "be equal parts pastor and politician. He was right! Every church I have served taught me that we had no plan or system for handling conflict."

One interviewee suggested that a better understanding of conflict would be helpful to clergy:

Interviewee: I entered into the ministry somewhat fearful of the dimension of conflict in the church. I am not somebody who loves fights and I have gotten into my fair share over the years. But I have come to recognize that if it's inevitable to have conflict and if you have an idea that conflict is that someone loses and must go away, you are not going to make it. However, if you understand that conflict is not the end of the world and that there still can be the possibility of family and unity, that is a wonderful lesson to learn. . . . I went to the church thinking that it was my job to fix everything that was wrong and handle every situation and always have something to say, and I had several points of helplessness. . . . I learned at those critical moments to trust the church.

Another pastor shared that conflicts often result from the minister's inability to listen to and understand the depth of pain—both his or her own pain and that of the congregation:

Interviewee: The year before I came, they [the congregation] had considered selling the church to keep the doors open. . . . eventually, we were going to build a parking lot. . . . The problem was we rented [the house on the lot where we were going to put the parking lot] to a family from another state who was here for their son to have a heart transplant. He was fourteen years old. That experience of waiting and praying with them for the transplant, its occurrence and completion were a source of extraordinary joy. The transformation in the child's appearance and energy and everything else was just so miraculous. And then came the rejection of that heart transplant. The anguish of that rejection and the pain of the family were hard on my congregation. This was a family that didn't hide anything; it was just all out there. . . . Whether it was an automobile accident, the loss of a job, divorce, the loss of a parent, I guess dealing with pain [openly] is one of the principle things that the congregation has taught me [in order to avoid conflict].

The importance of honesty and immediate communication was disclosed in one interview.

Interviewee: In the midst of a multi-million-dollar capital project, a legal/moral crisis emerged on our church staff. On a Monday night, I gathered the deacons to confront them with the news that the congregation would hear the next day. I had to walk them through everything from denial to being forgiving because everyone sins. In a three-hour session, we were finally able to reach the same point of the reality of implications and repercussions. Through emails and Sunday school classes making calls, the congregation gathered the next evening in the sanctuary. To have the sanctuary filled with people and to have 700 people show up on a Tuesday night was remarkable. We had an open forum conversation for two-and-a-half to three hours. In the end, what they said was, "Thank you for telling us the truth and not trying to protect anybody except for those who we all agree we need to protect. We need to protect children; we need to protect potential victims; we need to protect the integrity that we can protect and at the same time, we need to care about why we are here."

One pastor believes that the handling of conflict is easier when the pastor and leaders of the church are confident of the church's mission and stick to that plan with firm boundaries. He said,

Interviewee: There had been some patterns of unhealthy behavior which had been burning through that place for a long time. In fact, I realized there were always two fires burning: one was this vivacious Holy Spirit fire, and then there's this other fire of power and control and fear of manipulative people. These fires had been coexisting for a long time. When we realized what was up, we began to set boundaries about behavior. Here's how we love God and love each other. This is what it looks like and this is not what it looks like. . . . We've got a mission here which is to tend the fire of the Holy Spirit, and we need everyone to do that. . . . It was pretty terrifying at first. . . . So I called together a group of people and empowered them. Conflict would arise and we would refer to "this is our mission," or "this is our job." "We have all agreed to be involved in this mission. We want you to come along, but if you cannot, then that is your call, but we are going in this direction." After a while, a group of these people exited, so we pruned the church . . . it was absolutely necessary for new growth to happen. . . . The spirit of the congregation is healthy and vivacious. It's a place of team players. . . . the group feels liberated and energized. . . . What made it hard was because it tapped into my own issues and the way I was brought up. . . . Learning what your own issues are and then not projecting them onto others is really difficult.

The idea of the congregation and the pastor mirroring one another, thus explaining the sources of conflict, was highlighted in another interview.

Interviewee: Congregations are always in process, and congregations have taught me that the congregation is basically becoming what I am choosing to be. If I choose to be territorial, if I choose to be hierarchical, the congregation becomes that. If I choose to lead them from a standpoint of position, they will relate with me as a position; if I choose to be personable, they can relate to me as a person. . . . I believe one reason that some pastors leave the seminary so ill prepared is because they never really discovered their own personal identity. When they [i.e., these pastors] get into a congregation who is looking to the pastor to help them figure out who they are, they are just in constant conflict over role confusion.

Necessary and appropriate relational distance was also mentioned as a possible source of conflict.

One pastor spoke openly about being intentionally unavailable to his staff and congregation. He avoids conflict by not being present. His staff is expected to follow prescribed orders. Although physically absent, his absence did not eliminate conflict but created more tension between staff and congregants.

Interviewee: . . . a pastor must always remember that in the life of a congregation, [the pastor is not the lead sheep. He or she] is the shepherd. It is expedient for pastors (and staff ministers) to understand that if they allow themselves to become so absorbed into the relational life of the congregation as years go by . . . then they begin to think more as a member who represents or is an advocate for a slice of the pizza pie rather than making sure there are sausage and mushrooms on every slice of the pizza. I think sometimes that can be very lonely. The pastor begins to realize, "I am having to make a statement here and take a stance for those people with whom I am most closely identified personally. I have to remind them that their slice of pizza pie is not the [entire] pizza pie."

One pastor said that when he chose to send a proxy to church committee meetings, previous conflict began to subside.

Interviewee: Most of the decisions made by committees were what I could whole-heartedly support. The problems came in the process of getting to the decisions. So I asked our church administrator to meet with me and the chair of each committee before the announced time of the committee meeting. We would go over the agenda and what I would encourage the committee to consider. . . . Most of the time, when the committee reached a consensus, it was exactly where I would have been if I had been in the meeting. . . . It was just a refreshing thing for me. I did not have to do all that processing and I could give my focus to other things.

While conflict is rarely something for which we express thanks, one pastor wisely said, "We must be good stewards of conflict like you are a good steward of the other things you have—by managing it well and offering it up to God, and being a good chief and good boundary setter."

Interviewee: I think I started . . . with the assumption that if I can explain really clearly what I thought the truth was and show some kind of biblical justification for it, then everybody will end up agreeing with me [laughs]. This did not turn out being the case [laughs again]. So I guess the lesson in the abstract I would call to this is to recognize that there are very smart, very responsible people who, even when they understand your position fully, don't accept it. And so it's important not to lapse into the assumption that if people don't go along with you on something that either they are not very smart or they are not very good, that they are behaving without integrity. It is not true. When you do that it becomes harder, I think, to be negative about those who disagree with you. You want to affirm them as persons despite the disagreements. This may be truer in issues of theology/faith . . . because everybody, almost everybody, thinks they have the right theology or pretty close to it. . . . It's one of those subjects where people think they are all experts. So the result was a lot of differences.

If there is an issue, and there will be some—people taking a strong stand for the issue, people taking a strong stand against the issue— you try to give the best information to everyone on which they can base their decision. When the people have spoken, if they have said, "We do not want this," don't take it personally. If what you wanted to do is not what the people ended up wanting, the people have spoken; it's their church. It's not that the people have voted against you; they're voting against whatever hair-brained thing you have come up with. Occasionally, you will have a situation where a pastor will have a personality conflict with a member or they [just don't see eye-to-eye] and they never will. Go ahead and accept it; accept it for what it is, but you be there for them just like you're there for a person who's your next door neighbor and just does everything in the world for you and your family and you do the same for them. You always treat them the same. You're never ugly to them. You have to deal with the spirit of Christ.

A college professor of religion pointed out that pastors often fail to use the resources within their congregations that can be great tools for dealing with conflict.

Interviewee: Conflict in congregations is ill-understood and poorly addressed by most ministers. . . . And yet, at the very least, a pastor has, in most congregations, the people who are human resources managers, personnel managers, people who are teachers, people who are assistant principals, people who deal with conflict and have credentials in doing so that could provide some assistance in dealing with some of the trickier areas of the political life of the congregations.

At his interview of the search committee to a church, one pastor said to the calling committee,

Interviewee: I want you to know, and the entire congregation to know, that if we ever get to a point in any matter at which we cannot come to a Christian agreement, we can't sit down as brothers and sisters in Christ and work the thing out, don't ever worry about me hurting the church or taking anyone wherever I might be going, because I will be out of here before anyone notices. I promise you, based on my growing-up experiences. I would never do anything that will hurt this church. You have built it, you have been here all these years, and you will have to stay and clean up the mess if I decide to go. I'll try not to ever leave anything a mess. But you will have to clean it up and you're going to have to live with each other. You're going to have to love each other. You're going to have to get back together.

In addition, it is the pastor's role to provide and encourage experiences of resolution for conflict. One preacher preached on Matthew 5:23: "So if you are offering your gift at the altar, and there remember that your brother/sister has something against you, leave your gift there before the altar and go; first be reconciled to your brother/sister, and then come and offer your gift." The pastor then refused Communion to the congregation, saying that until they had made at least one attempt to put things right with their brothers and sisters, Communion would be closed. Meanwhile, the pastor would be available at the Table to dispense Communion once amends had been made— even if it took all day!

A seasoned pastor said that when prospective staff members are interviewed, he puts conflict right out front. He makes it clear that staff is in no way to be involved in the disruption of the congregation's fellowship.

Interviewee: I have no reluctance whatsoever when hiring a new staff person to say, "We've tried to show you everything that we are. We've tried to show you everything you will do. We told you about staff and the way we work together. Now, if you cannot totally support this, you tell me and the search committee, and we don't go any further. That's it. But if you make a commitment to support a church and the church's ministries, then if there gets to be a time that you cannot do that, the church is not going to move. You are going to move on. And as soon as you make it totally apparent that your agenda is something other than the agenda of the church, as of that time, you can no longer serve all the people of the church, and we'll need to make some changes."

And sometimes, the congregation just does the right thing.

Interviewee: I have had a few experiences in my life. About four years ago I was carjacked at gunpoint. It was a very traumatic experience. It ended up where a struggle went on and the carjacker ended up getting killed. It was one of those experiences where you tell folks you wish you never had to go through this. And it shook me, and it still does, even today. The church loved me through it.

(This pastor went to trial and was proven innocent due to eye-witnesses who came forward to testify that the pastor was unarmed while the assailant had a sawed-off shotgun.)

NOTE

1. Henri J. M. Nouwen, *The Wounded Healer: Ministry in Contemporary Society* (Doubleday & Company: New York, 1972) 96.

Chapter 5

THE CONGREGATION TEACHES GRACE

GRACE IN LOSS

Philip Gulley, a Quaker, and James Mulholland, a Baptist, are clergy partners for learning, reflection, and confiding much as Chris and I are. While they share the same seminary experience, often sitting next to one another in class, we share similarities in being raised in the church and serving as pastors in local congregations. (Chris was even the interim pastor of Baptist Church of the Covenant before I was called as its pastor.) Gulley and Mulholland in their book *If Grace Is True*, say they "cut their teeth" on theology that would follow this line of reasoning:

> God's grace was usually limited and qualified.
> God would be gracious if I accepted Jesus as my Savior.
> God would be gracious if I was baptized the right way
> God would be gracious if I attended the right church.
> God would be gracious if I prayed the right prayer.
> God would be gracious if I obeyed the right set of rules.
> God would be gracious if I got it right.

> I paid homage to God's grace while championing human freedom. Salvation was not dependent on God's decision to save me, but on my decision to accept Him. My righteousness determined my status and destiny. I controlled my destiny. I chose whether I was loved and accepted or hated and rejected. God's love was dependent upon my behavior. Grace was not a gift but a trophy.[1]

Seminary graduates may enter their first churches with similar thoughts of earned grace. It makes for a more reasonable, easily packaged theology that follows an "if/then" line of logic. We wonder then if ministers preach, teach and live with conditional grace, will they expect it in return? If so, the expectations we place on congregations are:

- A congregation's ability to give grace is limited and qualified.
- A congregation is grace-filled only if I visit in the nursing homes and hospitals.
- A congregation is grace-filled only if I pray the right words.
- A congregation is grace-filled only if I have the best ideas for committee work.
- A congregation is grace-filled only if the sermon gives evidence of scholarship.
- A congregation is grace-filled only if the budget is pledged every year.
- Only if . . . only if . . . and you fill in the blank.

Like the conclusion of Gulley and Mulholland, it would seem that a congregation's grace is conditional and dependent on the pastor's behavior(s). Grace then, is not a gift, but a trophy to be earned. From the parables of Jesus, alone, we find that God's grace is not logical or limited. After listening to the stories of our interviews, it would seem that our congregations may understand this better than professional clergy!

Two pastors set the stage for mutuality in ministry when each lost children. While their losses were under very different circumstances, each took the risk to talk openly with their congregations about their loss and grief. The trust they showed in breaking the silence and telling their personal stories sets an example for us all in believing the best of a congregation's willingness and ability to impart grace upon grace. The first story is from John Claypool, and the second is from William Sloane Coffin. Coffin does specifically mention how the membership of Riverside Baptist Church in New York City expressed grace to him and his family. Claypool sets the example of how to break the silence in the pulpit regarding personal challenges and, thus, trusting a congregation to receive and respond to the message with grace.

From John Claypool

[It was the] darkest single stretch of road I have ever been asked to travel. In July of 1968, I sat one Wednesday afternoon in the office of the chief hematologist of Children's Hospital in Louisville, Kentucky, and listened to words I could hardly comprehend: my eight-and-a-half-year-old daughter was suffering from acute lymphatic leukemia. . . .

We did everything in our power to counteract this terrible disease. Yet, in spite of it all, . . . my daughter lost her battle with leukemia . . . I was devastated by seeing her suffer as she did and then, at the end of it all, to die. . . .

It dawned on me that I had never deserved [my daughter] for a single day. She was not a possession to which I was entitled, but a gift by which I had been utterly blessed. And as that sense of her glowed in the darkness, I realized at that moment a choice stood before me. I could spend the rest of my life in anger and resentment because she had lived so short a time and so much of her promise had been cut short, or I could spend the rest of my life in gratitude that she had ever lived at all and that had the wonder of those ten grace-filled years. . . .

When one of my father's younger business associates was drafted into the army and needed a place to store his furniture, we ended up with an old green Bendix washing machine we could use in return for storage space. At the ripe old age of eleven, I was put in charge of the family laundry, so for the next four years, every Tuesday and Friday, I practiced the ritual of coming home from school, gathering up the dirty clothes, going down into the basement, and doing the laundry in the Bendix. It was one of those old-fashioned upright models with a plunger in the middle that created all kinds of wonderful configurations of soap bubbles. The wringer was two rubber rollers, operated by hand, and I can remember sticking my fingers between them to see just how far I could bear to go without cutting off circulation.

All of this to say that during those years, I developed a very affection-ate bond with the old green Bendix.

In 1945, the war came to an end and my father's business associate returned home. One day when I was at school, a truck pulled up and took all of his belongings from our basement, including the Bendix. No one told me, however, and since it was one of my regular wash days, I gathered up the clothes as usual and went down to the base-ment. To this day I can recall my sense of utter shock when I saw that gaping, empty space where the washing machine had once stood. I rushed back upstairs in a panic and announced loudly to my mother, "We've been robbed! Someone's stolen our washing machine!"

My mother took that occasion to teach me something very profound. "John," she said, "you must have forgotten how that washing machine got to be in our basement in the first place. It never belonged to us, and the fact that we ever got to use it at all was incredible good for-tune. Remember, John, you treat gifts differently from the way you treat possessions. When something belongs to you and it is taken away, you have a right to be angry. But when something is a gift and it is taken from you, you use that occasion to give thanks that it was ever given at all." . . .

It came to me that [my daughter] had been a part of my life in exactly the same way. She was a gift, not a possession. . . . To this day I believe that gratitude is the best of all the ways through the trauma of loss rather than a spirit of entitlement. It does not in any way elim-inate the intense pain and frustration that always accompany the work of rebuilding one's life in an entirely different context, but it does take away the feelings of anger and the conviction that a terrible injustice has been done, and it opens the way for thanksgiving. Gratitude also deepens our sense of trust, for we begin to believe that the One who gave us the good old days can be trusted to give us good new days as well.[2]

From William Sloane Coffin (1983)

As almost all of you know, a week ago last Monday night, driving in a terrible storm, my son Alexander—who to his friends was a real day-brightener, and to his family "fair as a star when only one is shining in the sky"—my twenty-four-year-old Alexander, who enjoyed beating his old man at every game and in every race, beat his father to the grave.

Among the healing flood of letters that followed his death was one carrying the wonderful quote from the end of Hemingway's *Farewell to Arms*: "The world breaks everyone and afterward many are strong at the broken places." My own broken heart is mending, and largely thanks to so many of you, my dear parishioners; for if in the last week I have relearned one lesson, it is that love not only begets love, it transmits strength. . . .

While the words of the Bible are true, grief renders them unreal. The reality of grief is the absence of God—"My God, my God, why hast thou forsaken me?" The reality of grief is the solitude of pain, the feeling that your heart's in pieces, your mind's a blank, that "there's not a joy the world can give like that it takes away" (Lord Byron).

That's why immediately after such a tragedy people must come to your rescue, people who only want to hold your hand, not to quote anybody or even say anything, people who simply bring food and flowers—the basics of beauty and life—people who sign letters simply, "Your broken-hearted sister." . . .

And that's what hundreds of you understood so beautifully. You gave me what God gives all of us—minimum protection, maximum support. I swear to you, I wouldn't be standing here were [I] not upheld.[3]

GRACE IN ALL THINGS

Just as Claypool and Coffin set the stage for pastors to open themselves up to the possibility of receiving grace from their congregations, so did several of the ministers who were interviewed for this project. Hear their stories.

Grace Despite Weakness

One pastor said forthrightly when responding to the question of what he had learned from his congregation, "Grace! That even with all my weaknesses and failure, they still love and accept me. One of my mentors used to say that as long as the congregation knows that you're doing your homework and you love them, you can basically get by with anything. You don't always have to be in the office, but you've got to be there when they need you. I think that's true. I think that pastors need to be visible in those crisis moments with people."

Grace in Moments of Failure

A pastor of a suburban congregation stated that his church taught him graceful failure. He grew up in a large congregation that was well managed by committees. At his first church, he suggested strengthening the committees and creating a church council. The congregation was patient and walked with him through that process, adjusting the constitution and bylaws. They tried it his way for eighteen months with few complaints. Then they came to him and said, "This is really not working." Being wise, he admitted that it was not working, and they went back to the old way of doing ministry together. He was grateful that they did not throw him out with the changes. "I learned how to fail happily but also learned that that was my introduction into the different ways of congregational life." He learned a valuable lesson. He experienced grace from his congregation.

Grace in Grief

Visible Grief

Interviewee: I believe the deaths of my sister and father allowed the congregation to see me grieve. I have been with so many of them in the last twenty-three years in similar situations. They saw in me that grief and tears and hurt and the pain of loss are okay to express. Preaching on the Sunday after my sister's death remains the most powerful preaching experience in my life . . . and for many in the congregation.

Shared Grief

Interviewee: My eight-year-old great-nephew was killed in a car accident three years ago. The event rocked our family severely. I had planned to preach for over six months on the Romans passage "what can separate us from God's love" (Rom 8:39). It became a text on the Sunday after the accident for me to deal with my grief and questions in the sermon. As a consequence, many in the congregation began to share stories with me of how tragic events had changed their lives and families and faith.

Grief in Suicide

Interviewee: When my sister committed suicide, the congregation did not know how to minister to me and my family. Of course, a few folks did, but most simply kept their distance—not knowing what to say or how to act. It was awkward for them, more so than for me. Years later, when my father died, the outpouring of love from the congregation overwhelmed me. I suspect it was the difference of having been their pastor for five years when my sister died and having been their pastor for twenty-plus when my dad died. Those were two very different experiences.

Balancing Grief and Leadership

Interviewee: Well, when we came to the church, our son was already born. And we were there I think for all of nine months when he died. And that affected the congregation in a profound way. In part because it was our son. He had a heart defect—a hole in his heart and some other things, too. We were living in another town when he was born, but quickly had to come here for surgery when he was only three weeks old. We had to come back for three surgeries total, and he died during the last one. When we came here for our son's surgeries, I got connected to the church through their services during the week. I began to develop a connection even before we were called here. That's why I think my coming was such a big deal for everyone, and continues to be. They already loved us by that time. We had been here for nine months when our son died. And they hurt for us. They were crushed, and we were crushed. I had to make a decision at that point on how to respond to my grief and our sense of loss because being the rector is public. I could, however, choose to what degree to be vulnerable with my grief. So I chose to be as open about the experience as was helpful. And what I mean by that is I did not feel it right to depend on the congregation to take care of my family and me in a dependent way. But it also would not be appropriate, I thought, to pretend to be invulnerable when, in fact, I was very vulnerable.

And so, somehow, I balanced that. Staying the leader and modeling trust in God in the middle of deep pain. . . . we let them [the congregation] give us pastoral care, and they did, and they do. They are good to us, in fact. But there's that complicated thing about leadership in that even when you are actually friends with people in your congregation, and that's rare, but when that happens, you're still the pastor. And that's okay. That's a good thing. But that's a balance. It's an art. I remember preaching about all this as it would come up in sermons—about being at the funeral home, because you know you had to go and identify the body. And that was horrible. And well, I did it. And I got off by myself at some point, blessedly, in the hallway, and I was trying to rehearse the basic facts. This is the kind of story I tell sometimes in sermons. It was overwhelming. "So, okay, you had a son and he died." . . . then there was the still small voice that said to me, "You have a son and he's passed from death into life." So, full of grief, there's some Life in that darkness. And that's the resurrection at work. So being able to share that with the congregation then and through the years is the way I've tried to model trust in hard times. Because I believe that God is making all things well and that resurrection is real and that this has been a way for me to proclaim the gospel. . . . It's an experience that has shaped us together. Our sense of [our son's] aliveness in God's presence, and being able to just say that and grieve and have hope all at once. That catches people at my parish. That experience and that story and talking about my son from the pulpit, that matters. And that's such a gift to me and to my wife.

Grace in Conflict

One pastor told of making a difficult deacon so angry that the deacon began to gossip about the pastor in the community. The pastor asked the chair of the deacons to join him in confronting the upset deacon. He explained,

Interviewee: I did everything the way you should do it. We shook hands, and he said that everything was fine. Then he went out, got mad, and left the church, taking not only his family but their friends as well, one of whom was my secretary! This church was only 120 members and 6 left. I was devastated. So I got the deacons together to tell them what happened. It was quiet for a minute and one of them said, "Well, preacher, we knew they were going to leave over something. We were just waiting to see what it was going to be." Then they blessed me, and we all went home.

Grace in Generosity

One pastor shared a wonderful story of serving in a rural community. He and his wife lived some distance from the church. The members of the church he served were struggling financially. Yet this pastor learned the value of grace through his members who did not have much. One of the members gave him and his wife vegetables to eat for the upcoming week. "I knew they couldn't afford it, and I knew they could barely afford food," the pastor said.

Interviewee: I said demonstratively, "Oh, you keep it. You can use it, and it's something you need to keep." He [the person giving us the food] said, "Do not deprive me of the joy of giving." And I cried. I learned that it is better to give rather than receive. It also means it is blessed to receive. One of the lessons that I learned was how to graciously receive when someone would give. That's what the congregation would do. Sometimes we feel like we're so self-sufficient until somebody comes along and makes us realize that we're not quite so self-sufficient after all. Sometimes pastors can become so slick and smooth that they are not aware of the need to act as sensitively towards people. I learned those lessons.

Grace in Disability

Interviewee: Our oldest son was diagnosed with muscular dystrophy, and the congregation came and they had prayer with us and expressed their concern for us in as many ways possible. That was a big influence and teaching experience for me of how congregations respond and have personal interactions with the pastor.

There were several members who were very much involved in our son's care. There was one lady in particular that asked if she could teach him to paint with his teeth, which would give him an outlet. He was very good with that. So every Friday I would take him by her house on my way to church and drop him off. She just lived two or three blocks from the church, and she would talk to him and teach him to paint and provided lunch for him. Then I would go by around lunchtime and eat with them, and then I would go back in the afternoon as I was leaving the office and would pick him up and take him home. They formed a beautiful and wonderful relationship. She and her husband were retired, and that was good for him; it also gave him an outlet because he did well in his painting.

The last day my son did those painting lessons was the last day that he lived. I picked him up. I had done a funeral that day, but I picked him up at the lady's house, and as we were getting his wheel-chair all situated, he looked at me and said, "You better not wear that suit to my funeral." I asked him what he was talking about. I had on a dark black suit, and he said, "You better not wear that suit to my funeral; it is going to be a happy home-going." And I said, "Listen young man, I don't have a bright red suit to wear." That initiated our conversation, though, and we talked about fear of death and dying on the way home. As we were backing into the garage I said, "Son, are you afraid to die?" He said, "No, I trusted Jesus a long time ago and I am not afraid to die, but my only regret is that you have spent so much time at the church and I am afraid Mother will be left alone." I said, "I give you my word, I will take care of your mother if something happens to you." I have always felt guilty about this and still do, but I made that kind of investment in the life of my congregation at the expense of my family, which is not good. My congregation is not aware of that, or they didn't notice it, but I tried to be there when they had a crisis in their life and they needed a pastor, but I should have spent more time with my family; I should have budgeted my time better with my family. I don't think the congregation would have complained if I had taken a little more time with my family, and so it was not the congregation's fault.

Then when our son passed away . . . immediately upon hearing the news, church members began to come and clean around the house and dust things and pick up things and cook meals and bring food and just greet guests and answer the phone and any number of things. They stayed there the whole time, but they also were concerned about us and our feelings, so they gave us time to be alone so we could grieve in our way too. I think the way that they ministered to me was an important teaching experience. I think being a pastor or shepherd should be a mutual thing.

Mutual Grace

Through their collective years of serving local congregations, Gulley and Mulholland have evolved in their understanding of grace. They propose:

> I can remember many altar calls where the preacher reminded us that 'man is destined to die once and after that to face judgment' (Hebrews 9:27). I still agree with that order—death, then judgment. Yet even this sequence makes it clear that death doesn't have the final word. The judge does.
>
> . . . In the heavenly court, there will be no conflict of interest. God's love will influence his judgment. He will not don his black robes and forget who we are. He may chastise. He may express his disappointment. He may even punish. But his final word will be a redeeming word of grace.[4]

Our greatest hope is that as seminarians become seasoned ministers of the parish, that the influence, witness and presence of their parishioners will evolve into a new understanding of grace. Grace not just for pastors to remind and give to their charges, but genuine grace that pastors may gratefully receive from the membership of Christ's church.

NOTES

1. Philip Gulley and James Mulholland, *If Grace is True* (San Francisco: Harper, 2003) 104.

2. John Claypool, "The Wound of Grief," *Mending the Heart* (Chicago: Cowley Press, 1999) 63–66.

3. William Sloane Coffin, "Alex's Death," *The Riverside Years* (Louisville: Westminster John Knox, 2008) 3–6.

4. Gulley and Mulholland, *If Grace Is True*, 121.

Chapter 6

The Congregation Teaches Pastoral Care

In his book *Generation to Generation: Family Process in Church and Synagogue*, the late Edwin H. Friedman focused on clergy and family systems.[1] Those interviewed frequently cited this work as the most helpful information they had received, and if they had been able to return to seminary, they desired further study in this area. One person even quoted a bumper sticker about this work that read, "Rabbi Jesus saved my soul. Rabbi Friedman saved my ass!" The introduction of Friedman's noble work sets the tone for some of our discoveries as we interviewed clergy:

> For decades I have listened to the anguished tales of ministers, rabbis, priests, and nuns as they relate their experiences about entanglements with members of their congregations, conflicts within their religious hierarchies, and ambivalence toward their relatives. The extraordinary similarity of these stories, despite their different contexts, has led me to two conclusions. One is that the family is the true ecumenical experience of all humankind. The second is that what most unites all spiritual leaders is not a set of beliefs or practices but the factors that contribute to our stress.[2]

Friedman's thesis confirms what the interview process revealed: "All clergymen and clergywomen, irrespective of faith, are simultaneously involved in three distinct families whose emotional forces interlock: the families within the congregation, our congregations, and our own."[3] We did not hear specific stories about families (i.e., clans) within the congregation although we, as well as others, often experience this connected system within the larger church family. We did hear stories that speak to the pastor's specific family and the congregation as family. Those stories follow.

THE CONGREGATIONAL FAMILY . . .

Cares for Special Needs

Interviewee: There is a man in our congregation that has special needs. He takes Communion four or five times every Sunday, and you are, of course, only supposed to take it once. What he will do is, he will take Communion from every station. I can't tell you the number of times that I see people say, "He has already had Communion four times!" Isn't it funny? Sometimes I have him help me serve Communion and he hugs everybody. . . . We really need him, because in a community like ours where everything, even the people, are beautiful and perfect, there is also this man. . . . He has become my idol/mentor.

Cares for One Another

Interviewee: On New Year's Eve, I injured my hand badly on a chain saw. I had to have surgery. My first day with my cast on, I came out from the service and a teenager came up to me and asked the question that I am sure everyone had been wanting to ask.

"What did you do to your arm?" I said that this was a man's injury and I did it with a chain saw.

He said, "You did that with a chain saw? Well, you and me, we have something in common."

I said, "We have something in common?" He said that he had busted his butt on a skateboard and his elbow had cracked in four places and it hurt like hell.

I said, "This hurt like hell."

He said, "I promised to Jesus, if you let me out of this, I will never get back on a skateboard again."

I said, "Really?"

He said, "Yeah, I learned a lot from it."

I said, "What did you learn from it?"

He said, "I learned sure as hell never to promise anything to Jesus again that I couldn't keep!"

Another minister describes members of the congregation who simply "take care of each other":

Interviewee: I have a member who earns a moderate income and has two children. [There is a male member] who makes a lot of money. When he heard her talking about her situation, he stepped forward to pay for her children to go to camps all summer. It was all done quietly. They just take care of each other.

FAMILY . . .

Is Given Unique Gifts

Interviewee: I think that churches would like to teach their pastors that there are no first or second or third class members of the church. They're all the same. Now they may not have the same level of gifts, but every one of them can do something that is of equal importance in the kingdom work.

Is Forgiving

Interviewee: At my first church, there were more people buried in the church graveyard that had died by violence than those who had died by natural causes. It was in that church that I baptized a descendent of the McCoys of the famous Hatfields and McCoys. He shot his father to death and beat a neighbor to death. The wisdom from the congregation was, "Don't even stop by his house." But I did one day and found that he was very lonely for someone to visit with him. He was very eager to set things right in his life. The morning he joined the church, he could not look when the church voted to receive him. They did. I think I learned along with them that a congregation has to be able to forgive and integrate persons into the community of faith who have otherwise been ignored.

Is Loved

Interviewee: In the pastorate, every time you lose a person to death, and they go on to be with our Lord, there's a certain kink that has been knocked out of your armor. Knocked off your very soul and you know it can never be replaced. Someday I will be able to feel the level of appreciation and thankfulness for every one of those lives, but not until I get to the point where every one of those losses stops hurting. I see it from the youngest to the oldest. I am grateful for everything ever done, grateful for deep faith, grateful for all that they have brought to the ministry. But I have felt deep loss with all of them. And that, to me, is where I have felt hurting in being a pastor that I never thought was possible.

Is Challenging

Interviewee: One thing I am most grateful to have learned from a congregation is how to love my enemies. I thought I knew how to love my enemies, but then we had to visit them in the hospital, and then we had to do their funerals, and then everyone else around you loves them . . . even though they are a pain in the behind, and everybody knows it . . . still everyone loves them. You have to learn to love those people too and it is quite a gift and quite a lesson to learn.

Is Human

Interviewee: I was visiting with a woman whose child had died, and she said, "Reverend, you will never understand what it's like to lose a child." She had not heard about the miscarriages in our family and that my wife had not really dealt with the loss and all that goes with that. . . . And so I said, "Mrs. [name], I do know that story and I know that experience. I know what it's like to have great hopes and then for whatever God reasons, it's not going to be fully actualized." And her mouth kind of dropped. I learned that you don't say to another individual, . . . "You don't know what it's like" because you [never know what they have been through until they tell you].

Is Grateful for Leadership

Interviewee: When I had been at my church for only a few months, a beloved staff member died suddenly early one Sunday morning. When I got to church, I knew I had to tell the church. But before that, prior to Sunday school, I called a meeting of some of the key leaders in the church to discuss how to break the news. That group showed remarkable wisdom in a crisis moment, and we handled the situation gracefully. After the sermon that I preached on responding to loss through grief (not the sermon I had prepared), one of the leading members told me, "We're going to get through this all right. Thanks for leading us." Our shared moment of sorrow allowed us to also experience a shared moment of healing.

Is Joyful

Interviewee: One of the church members had been injured in a mining accident and was living on a meager subsidy. Every drop of water that came to his house, he carried a half-mile in a bucket. This man had the most vivacious Christian spirit of anyone in that church. The only thing he knew to do and to do well was to come stoke the furnace on Sunday mornings to warm the place. He did it with great joy. I think it gave me my first glimpse of how wonderful Christian individuals can be given the opportunity to serve.

THE MINISTER'S PERSONAL FAMILY

While most of those interviewed were married and had a family, two of the interviews dealt with being single ministers. One single pastor referred to it as a gift and a calling unto itself, much as Paul did in the New Testament. Another said the following:

Interviewee: . . . it's been an interesting thing for me. My family of origin, my parents, still live here, and I have siblings who have children who are very important to me. The congregation has been largely very gracious about those relationships and understanding that I need to go and be a part of that family. My mother has been very ill a few times and people have been gracious and supportive of whatever time you need [to be with family]. The other side of that, however, is because I'm not married and have no children, there's this other feeling that creeps up in the congregation (and I work with another associate, who is a female and who is unmarried and has no children) that means you don't have a life outside the church. And so you should be expected to be there all the time, for anything, and why do you need four weeks of vacation. You don't have a family to go and do things with. So it's a sort of an interesting flip on that because I do have family and a lot of friends that I think of as family in many ways. Figuring out how to protect that freedom and need to have time away and apart has been interesting given that there is that sentiment in the congregation too.

Keeping Family a Priority

The health and well-being of the minister and the minister's family is vitally important for the health of the congregation. Congregations should do all they can to support the minister and the minister's family in order to create and maintain a healthy environment. As we conducted this research, we wondered whether the church is a safe place for the pastor and the pastor's family.

With a general question about families, we combined the answers of those interviewed and discovered that between them they represented more than 634 years of marriage and that these marriages produced more than 83 children. There were admissions of divorce and remarriage. Clergy also served a combined total of more than 900 years in ministry, including service as associates, chaplains, university and seminary professors, denominational leaders, and other professions where the minister served in bi-vocational careers.

Those interviewed have served across the spectrum of congregational geography: urban, suburban, and rural. As these pastors have moved, responding to calls from congregations, so have their families. Whether by design or not, families become a part of the systemic life of each congregation. One clergyperson, speaking of her family, said, "My family accepted that pastoring a church is a family job. And I'm grateful to them that they did so willingly. I felt very supported by my family and [the church supported my family]."

For pastors/ministers to be successful, their families have to be a priority. One pastor commented that the congregation being served wanted him to keep his family first. "Now I don't mean that everybody every day is going out of their way to make sure that I get four to five weeks vacation a year to spend with family," he said. "That's not true. But they do want me to have that as priority. And, of course, I've also called on [my congregation]. I've made that clear and they have supported that."

Being understanding of the spoken and unspoken expectations placed on their spouses as well as themselves often makes pastors' work go better. Ministers recounted the role their respective spouses played:

Interviewee: . . . her purest experience in that role [of minister's wife], she learned early that people will use her as a back door to me in terms of passing on information or trying to get information and stuff like that. She would get cornered frequently by people who were trying to pass on a message or "wheedle" some information out. But she learned to maneuver that and also learned to develop her own ministry. She's excellent. She has always . . . taken it seriously, not just as a lay Christian sitting in the pew.

Another interviewee described the importance of setting boundaries in keeping family a priority:

Interviewee: I was a member of a priest's family growing up, and now I have a bishop's family. I think, too often, clergy families suffer from lack of time with their clergyperson—male or female. The church can be a demanding mistress, often taking you away from your family. I certainly felt that my father was somewhat removed from my life. I was a lot more involved in my son's life than my father was in mine. Weekends are a big issue. Not having free weekends. If your kids go to school Monday through Friday and you work the weekends, what quality time do you have? So I try very hard to say to my clergy that you must have a day off during the week for sanity and family time.

I've tried to make family a first priority. My rule is that healthy clergy make healthy churches. And healthy clergy have to have healthy families and good boundaries—and Sabbath time. Boundaries are the key issue. I've seen clergy with no boundaries and I've seen clergy with hard boundaries and neither one works. People without boundaries are sacrificing their families and themselves. I met a guy once who came in and told his church that he would not do Saturday weddings except once every two months and the other clergy would do the others. He also announced that he would not take calls after 5:00. That's no way to establish boundaries. Boundaries need to be internal. But don't tell people your boundaries because they will feel like you shut them out.

Pastors' busy and hectic schedules often present a challenge to personal time with their families. Clergy are often over-committed and workaholics. Perhaps this is true because there is little in the way of visible results from their labors. One pastor explains,

Interviewee: A carpenter can build a garage and step back and say, "Look at what I have done." As a priest, it's difficult to look back and see what I have done. So much of [ministry] is intentional—touching people's lives with something you say or do—it can make such a difference, but you don't even know it. It's a lot of giving but not a lot of seeing results. But the fact is that the results of the lives you touch and the things you say and the modeling of the Christian life is so important.

Another pastor found a solution to the busy schedule in the way he kept his calendar.

Interviewee: Before Blackberrys and laptops, we used the old Day-Timer system usually for every part of planning for the day. Young pastors need to realize that being a pastor is not easy, and I also learned how important it was to have accountability to the staff, accountability to the patrons, to my family. I learned how important it was to design family time and put family events on a calendar so if someone says, "Can we have a committee meeting Thursday night?" I can say, "I'm sorry. I have a commitment. I have a commitment to go see my son play baseball." Make sure it's no less important than a committee meeting. I learned a lot about family time from the congregation and from individuals.

Support staff members often provide the buffer for ministers to carve out time with their families.

Interviewee: One office manager said to me, "Pastor, it's my job to protect you." The language itself sounded rather unclear. But I've come to understand that she meant all the good in the world in terms of protecting me from overload and from not sacrificing time at home with my wife and sons. She was really concerned, as all of my staff persons are, the older I become. They were concerned with me not [becoming so busy in ministry that I neglected the important things of life].

One final example captures what many of our interviewees may have been thinking (emphasis added).

Interviewee: My family is very important to me. I need to cherish my family. I shouldn't put the needs of the congregation in front of the needs of my family. Because at the end of the day, I don't want my children to say I care more about the church than I care about my own family. *I've always said that my first ministry is my family.*

The Separation of Church and Spouse

The minister's spouse can either enhance or ruin a minister's effectiveness by their support or lack thereof. Many talked about the role(s) their spouses played in the church.

Interviewee: When I was interviewed by the Pastor Search Committee, my husband was asked what he had to bring to the table. We laughed as he said, "I don't play the piano and doubt that I would win the church bake-off!" His sense of humor has won him the beloved title of "Big Momma" in the congregation. It is a sign of deep affection for the ways he has loved the members and the ways he supports me.

One pastor said the following clarifying conversation took place at his call interview:

Interviewee: "Now, let me be sure exactly who you're hiring for this position."

The committee shook their heads and said, "Well, we're hiring you."

I said, "Does that mean you're not hiring my wife?"

And they said, "No, that's right."

And I said, "Don't ever forget it. I will be the one who's a member of this staff; she will not be. We have our children and she takes care of them. She takes care of the home in ways that she needs to. I do the same in ways that I need to. But I will never back up to you to get my check. I'll earn every penny of it and more. I give you my word. But she's not hired, so don't be calling on her for everything that you feel like needs to be done at the church."

We learned that the participation of spouses takes many diverse forms.

Interviewee: I believe the congregation tells me that my family is important to me—that the help of my family is important and my relationship with my family, which usually translates into time that I can spend with my family, [is] important. What the congregation also says is that my family is not me—that we're separate. For example, my wife does not come to worship. She sings in the choir at another church, but she comes on Wednesday nights. She's there for special occasions. She's involved and helpful, but they don't see her on Sunday mornings in worship. Of course, they don't see either of my sons because they are away at school.

Ministers who have converted as adults may have spouses who never dreamed they would find themselves married to a minister.

Interviewee: To me, family commitments are absolute, and they have priority over careers, or, if you call it vocation, over vocational commitments. I steadily took a position with my students that if you're hurting your family, quit doing this and do something else. One of the students I most admired was a convert in adult life. He had been married for a long time. He was a riverboat captain, interestingly, and could work one day a week and be a whole lot better off than any of the faculty or students. He would guide these ships up the Mississippi River on Saturday.

His wife did not want to be a minister's wife. Now, I would guess that nine out of ten of my students would have said, "Hey, God called me, you have to do this." And then there would have been a divorce. He didn't. He talked to her. She was a practicing Christian who simply acknowledged that she did not sign on to this. And she didn't. They had been married for thirty years and she never signed on to be a minister's wife, and she was savvy enough to know there was a price to be paid there and she didn't intend to pay it. This is what he did. I've always admired him. He said, "Okay, I do feel that God has called me to ministry, but I will simply continue to do this captain's stuff that I do." Then he became the president of the Gideons group in New Orleans, and in that role, he was invited to preach. He would sign up to be available to speak in churches. Now it would basically be the same sermon over and over again to support Gideons and the Bible distribution and all that. But the point is, he had a ministry and got to know the people who are in leadership in church. Obviously, one Sunday at a time, but that's the form his ministry took because he put his marriage ahead of his calling. And that seems right to me. That's a contestable idea, I understand. But it seems right to me. I always urge students to do that. I don't want to go too far here, but families are not to be sacrificed up. . . . But among me and my students, spouses and children both can get a bad deal because of a husband [or wife] trying to follow his [or her] call.

Family Gives a Different Perspective . . .

Family members are often supportive of ministers in their family. However, they can bring their understanding of what they perceive ministry to be within a given context. And, as they reflect upon their personal experiences in ministry, they may bring a set of questions and criticisms into the family member's ministry. The following excerpts tell the stories of family honesty and unique perspective:

Interviewee: One of my favorite stories about the early days [of my ministry] involves my mom and dad. They always went to big Baptist churches. Our average attendance was about twenty or so. But they wanted to be supportive, so they came down the first Sunday or so that I was there to participate in the worship service. My dad was a self-made kind of guy who was very plainspoken. I was standing in the back of the sanctuary, and they were sitting in the pews. I could see them looking around. Then, I heard him say out loud, "Where are all the people?"

Interviewee: My grandfather was a pastor of local churches for forty-one years. So ministry is a part of my family's history. In fact, my dad was a little bit antagonistic towards the idea of my going into ministry. I think because he saw a lot of the negative side of ministry. . . . When I started talking about ministry, he started talking about law school. "You know, why don't you do that, then you can take care of this 'hobby' later on."

CARING FOR THE MINISTER

Some pastors may tend to neglect the reality that they are parishioners, members of the local congregations they serve, and thus entitled to pastoral/congregational care when they are ill or experiencing challenges. One pastor shared the story of being diagnosed with cancer. He openly told his congregation about the diagnosis and described the process his team of physicians suggested to address the cancer. From the initial announcement, the congregation responded with an outpouring of loving care, concern, and support. The pastor reported,

Interviewee: I wasn't shocked, maybe just overjoyed that so many members were present early that morning of the surgery. There were more than twenty-five members present, and some stayed with my wife throughout the day. Their presence not only benefited me personally but was a witness to others who were in the waiting room. I felt special, cared for, and loved. I did not see other pastors present or other congregants with their members. But there we were, huddled in prayer. Even a non-member, who was having surgery, joined the circle.

This pastor reported receiving many cards, phone calls, and a few visitors during the recovery at home. "It is a wonderful feeling to know that the congregation you minister to is capable of ministering to the minister!" he said. When asked why he thought members responded so graciously, he replied, "Maybe they have been encouraged to treat all people with kindness and compassionate, caring love. Or, perhaps, I'm the pastor and they felt that their response was the right thing to do. Initially, I thought some came just to be nosy, but that quickly dissipated as I looked in their eyes and could see their sincerity."

Another minister shared the frustration of serving and being supportive of the needs of her family. After serving congregations for several years, her children voiced concern about not being able to attend football games or not being stable long enough to establish meaningful friendships. The minister requested to move back to her hometown. She was sent to a church where the current pastor was trying to leave. Becoming disillusioned by the placement and by events such as one parent dying, the other parent becoming ill and the need to find employment. She responded to the disillusionment by leaving her denomination for approximately three years. She did not attend church. She completely dropped out.

As fate would have it, she became ill. Here is the conclusion to her story.

Interviewee: When I got well enough to come back to church, it was my home church that said, "Reverend, we love you." They began to minister to me. . . . It was the people who ministered to me and said they loved me and wanted me there with them. They nourished me back. They represented to me God's grace. As I was restored to wholeness, God was saying to me, "Yeah, they left you and deserted you, but I never left you." I guess that's why I love that group of people. They just minister to me so much. I felt like I wasn't worthy to read the Scripture or to minister to them, but they said, "Come on, teach Bible study." Right after that, the pastor became ill and I started teaching the Bible study. And they were coming out to Bible study, which forced me to read even more. . . . When it was time for the annual report, there was a lot of growth. We had not fallen apart. We had grown!

Another pastor remembered her daughter being accepted to a school with a high tuition, and the family couldn't afford it. Some congregants got together and made sure that they could afford the tuition.

While many of the stories of congregations offering generous care to their ministers, one pastor wished that the congregation had been more responsive during a personal crisis: "In those twenty-one [years of serving as the pastor of a congregation], my mother died and I got a flower from the church. My wife was in the hospital several times and no one offered to pay any of my medical bills. My last child was premature. I got nothing. But still, there is their want of me to be full-time. And I think, 'Well, if you want me full-time, do something.'"

Another pastor wished that his time with his family had been more respected. He wrote,

Interviewee: Getting away for vacations with family is often interrupted. I was unable to take the family with me on a family vacation and not be called back. It happened for at least twenty-five years. Every vacation. And that was unfair to them, but I could not help it. We didn't have anyone else to handle it. I didn't come back unless I absolutely had to. If I could come back, which I did many times, I would come back to rejoin the family on vacation. That's not right!

One pastor summarized his view of family quite succinctly: "To realize that the pastor's family is just as fallen—and just as redeemed—as other families was a discovery that was a gift."

NOTES

1. Edwin H. Friedman, *Generation to Generation: Family Process in Church and Synagogue* (New York: Guilford Press, 1985).

2. Ibid., 1.

3. Ibid.

Chapter 7

Conclusions

From the outset, it has not been our purpose to degrade or diminish the work of seminaries. We both have deep appreciation for our seminary experiences and the education we received there. It is our objective, however, to illustrate for educational institutions, their students and graduates, and local congregations that seminaries are only a beginning point for learning, personal growth, and the development of professional skills. While the local pastor needs an active appetite to continue to learn, local congregations should serve as equal partners in teaching and learning along with the seminary and pastor. In our interview process, we heard specific suggestions for how seminaries, congregations, and pastors might develop their conversations for mutual learning. The ideas of those interviewed follow. Where stories were available, they were included.

THE SEMINARY

• Continue to strive for excellence in the classroom with professors who have a working knowledge of the local church as well as their subject matter.
• Foster an appreciation of and offer opportunities for continuing education, such as lectionary study groups, lectures, and seminars.
• Develop a "think tank" where ministers can come and be heard. Many pastors left the interviews expressing appreciation simply for having been heard. Many said that they had never stopped long enough to think about the topics introduced, and most were grateful for the opportunity to consider some of the major events of their ministry careers. Perhaps in compiling these stories, seminaries might get a richer picture of what seminarians need as they prepare for church work.

• Maintain contact with graduates/alumni for support and encouragement other than financial solicitation.
• Develop programs/seminars for churches in which congregations are taught skills for receiving a new pastor, conflict resolution, and the importance of continuing education for ministers.
• Require more extensive placements and internships, even one- to two-year internships. Several pastors spoke of the significance and effectiveness of internships and fieldwork on their practice of ministry. One pastor said, "My denomination requires four years of internship that we used to call 'In Place.' It consisted of three years of academic study and one year of full-time service in a church. I was pretty well rounded and prepared when I graduated."

Interviewee (a religion professor): My Senior Seminar and Congregational Ministries (college-level course) is 180 hours in the field with a very experienced mentor with credentials and at least seven years of pastoral or other ministerial experience. And with that also came a colloquium. The students who are participating in different internship settings in order to model a peer group and the power of a peer group outside of the particular ministerial setting—I think those things are helpful. I think in some instances that the process of an internship for students who are interested in ministry at the undergraduate level determines whether or not they go on successfully in ministry.

• Provide each graduate with a mentor in ministry by giving and/or assigning the graduate to a pastor in the area in which they are leaving the seminary to serve.

Interviewee: There was a senior pastor in the neighborhood. He was twenty-five miles away, and I went to him for advice when I became a pastor.
    At the divinity school, they had a program called "Minister in Training." It was a covenant agreement between the student and the church. The church was aware that they were a training ground or a training school for the . . . divinity student. So I worked about an hour away [from the seminary]. . . . The pastor there was superb—an

excellent preacher, exegetical preacher, a superb pastor among his people. The program self-consciously allowed us to do everything that the pastor did; we were not just assigned to the youth group. So we went out sometimes three days a week and shadowed him in everything that he did. And there were just so many insights, just the pastoral style, going to a person's home and at the conclusion of the meeting not saying, "Well, let's have a prayer," but "Would you like me to have a prayer, Ms. Wagner?" Just little nuanced ways of being with people were tremendously helpful. And the people at the church were aware of their commitment to this relationship; they were part of the covenant also. They helped school us in how to be a pastor. I often used to say, I learned more in that one year . . . than the other three academic years.

THE CONGREGATION

• Provide specific and clear job descriptions that outline specific expectations.
• Provide, discuss and allow for competitive salaries, benefits (medical, dental, eye, and disability), vacation time, continuing education and counseling services.
• Be supportive of family time and vacation.
• Clearly communicate any expectations of the "first family."
• Conduct annual evaluations and reviews with clear achievable objectives for the next year.
• Do not be afraid to seek outside help when there is conflict. Many organizations offer help to ministers and to churches.[1]
• Consider and implement the benefits of hiring seminarians/Pastoral Interns/Residents.

Perhaps the best selling point of such teaching opportunities is that the *residents* are not the only ones learning. Learning becomes reciprocal so that new wisdom and confidence about pastoral practice is generated. New resources create positive energy on both sides of this fence. Recognizing that the practice of ministry creates the most positive environment for the formation of pastoral leaders, graduates may want to research and pursue programs such as the Transition into Ministry initiative sponsored by the Lily Foundation since 1999. Daniel Aleshire says of such initiatives,

> Congregational and other ministry settings create the environment for a different kind of learning. They help students learn to think more clinically, administratively, organizationally, and interpersonally. These settings don't teach novice ministers how to "apply" what they learned in school. Rather, these environments evoke different "intelligences" and students engage in a different kind of intellectual work. It is intellectual work that deals with the kind of wisdom that accrues from practices, from skills that get better with repetition and reflection, from perceptions that are informed and enriched by coaching. These lessons are not learned well in a classroom; in fact, they *can't* be learned in a classroom.[2]

INDIVIDUAL PASTORS

• Attend continuing education seminars and conferences on an annual basis. One pastor said, "I found the congregation to be willing to read books with me and then to talk about them. They sent me to conferences and asked me questions. I guess they saw sending me off to get this continued learning as a way of enriching themselves, enriching the congregation."

• Keep a professional counselor on retainer. Just because your parishioners "go crazy," doesn't mean you have to! A pastor told us, "When I graduated from seminary, I started seeing a therapist in my denomination, and saw him for over twelve years once a week and sometimes twice a week. And I think that was life-saving for me to have that relationship, in dealing with everything that had to do with being pastor of a church on my own."

• Keep reading.

• Maintain a Sabbath.

Interviewee: I have intentionally set apart a Sabbath from every Monday noon to every Tuesday noon because my secretary is in the office Monday morning, and I've got to be in the church. I don't have a whole day that I can do it. I take that time as my Sabbath, and only do things then that draw me closer to God. . . . I always ask myself, "What about this is bringing me closer to God? How does that affect who I am? Where do I see God at work in this?" It's been incredible. . . . I work seriously in that time. I have a little room I've set up in my house that's big enough to have a twin bed at the end and a chair and a table where I set up a little altar. I can sit in there and pray. The other thing that's happened is I can write there.

• Receive annual/bi-annual medical exams.
• If your seminary doesn't pair mentors with graduates, seek out a mentor on your own.
• Be a mentor.
• Develop a support group of peers that goes across denominational lines OR develop friendships outside of the church. Mainly, find a circle where you can "spit, cuss, and chew."
• Enroll in clergy wellness programs offered by groups such as The Clergy Wellness Program of the Episcopal Diocese of California or The Resource Center for Pastoral Excellence at Samford University (see appendix 3 and 4).

Perhaps the best lesson from all the data we accumulated comes from the uniqueness of the first pastorate experience. Humble and willing to continue to be taught, the pastor forms lasting skills that are characteristic of his or her ministry throughout a lifetime. Should the pastor continue in the mode of student, constantly willing to learn and be taught, and should each congregation continue to answer the high calling of co-learner and patient teacher, then there is indeed hope for the future of the church and its ministers. If all of us could recognize that we are works in progress despite our shortcomings and failures, then together we are stronger and have the objective not only to keep issuing the call of God to each generation but also to give ministers and congregations the room they need to come to life and flourish. Therefore, we close with five pastors' words of encouragement:

• Ministry is a two-part invention: there has to be a living dialogue and vulnerability in the relationship. A priest is only as good as his or her ability to be with people in an open way.

• I don't know if I've done as much good for them as they have done for me.

• Be constantly aware that it is God's church, not ours.

• Pastors must not lose sight of the fact that the minister's invitation to step into his or her members' lives at critical, private moments is a privilege and not an imposition.

• You've got to love the people. If you can't love them, you need to leave.

Notes

1. Check out The Alban Institute, 131 Elden St., Suite 202, Herndon VA 20170, www.alban.org; or Center for Congregational Health, Medical Center Blvd., Winston-Salem NC 27157-1098, congreg@wfubmc.edu.

2. Daniel Aleshire, *Earthen Vessels: Hopeful Reflections on the Work and Future of Theological Schools* (Grand Rapids: Eerdmans, 2008).

QUESTIONNAIRES

WHAT CONGREGATIONS TEACH THEIR PASTORS

We've included the questionnaire we used with our interviewees so readers may see how we gathered our information.

Individual Questionnaire

Name
Describe your family
Seminary attended
Date of graduation
Degree obtained
Particular area of study

As you reflect on your seminary experience, what were the most valuable tools for ministry you received?

If you were to return to seminary, in what areas would you like to receive further study?

What are some challenges in ministry for which seminary did not prepare you?

Place of current or most recent service:

How many years served as pastor?

List in consecutive order your places of service:

What lessons has your congregation taught you?

There are many societal issues that show themselves in congregations (i.e., HIV/AIDS, abuse in the home, substance abuse, mental illness, issues of sexuality). What does your congregation teach you about these issues? How have these lessons affected/changed/improved pastoral care?

How did your congregation teach you?

What are the most valuable lessons a congregation can teach their pastor?

What are the best ways a congregation can teach their pastors?

How would you teach this lesson in a seminary setting to students?

Tell a memorable experience with a congregation

What does your congregation teach you about your family?

Has a personal event in your life caused a moment of shared learning with a congregation?

Describe your support system that feeds your spirit

What Congregations Teach Their Pastors

Faculty Questionnaire

Name

Seminary/graduate school attended

Date of graduation

Degrees obtained

Particular area of study/or subjects currently teaching

How many years served as pastor . . . serving now while being a faculty member?

What are the lessons your students need to be taught in order to be successful in ministry?

There are many cultural issues that affect one's ministry/pastoral care (HIV/AIDS, abuse in the family, mental illness, substance abuse, etc.). Give a priority list of issues students need information about/experience with in order to be effective ministers.

What are the most valuable lessons a congregation can teach their pastor?

What are the best ways a congregation can teach their pastors?

How would you teach this lesson in a seminary setting to students?

What is the role of a seminary in supporting students and their families?

What does seminary teach a pastor about the importance of family connectedness?

Has a personal event in your life caused a moment of shared learning with a congregation?

Tell a memorable experience with a congregation . . . yours and/or a student's.

Describe your support system that feeds your spirit

How are these support systems encouraged among faculty and students and then, ultimately, taken into the pastoral realm?

Release and Consent Agreement

In return for valuable consideration, the undersigned, _____, (hereinafter "Releaser") hereby gives his/her consent to be interviewed Sarah J. Shelton and/or Christopher M. Hamlin. Releaser understands that all or part of the interviews may be recorded and notes may be taken. Releaser relinquishes and waives any and all rights and interests of any kind which he/she might otherwise have in any publications, audio or video recordings, notes or memoranda generated during or as a result of the interviews.

Releaser further grants exclusive permission for Sarah J. Shelton, Christopher M. Hamlin, The Center for Pastoral Excellence at Samford University, and their publishers (hereinafter collectively referred to as "Releasees") to publish or cause to be published, in their sole discretion, all or any portion of the material generated during the interviews, with the sole exception of the Releaser's name. Releaser does not consent to the use of his/her name by Releasees in any publication produced by or for the Releasees. The Releasees agree that they will not identify the Releaser by name in any publication.

Releaser further releases, discharges, and holds harmless the Releasees, their publishers, agents, employees, designees, heirs, and assigns, from any claims or liability, in tort or contract, for any damages which may arise from the publishing of any material generated during or as a result of the interviews of Releaser.

_____   _____

DATE   DATE

_____   _____

RELEASOR PRINTED NAME   WITNESS PRINTED NAME

_____   _____

RELEASOR SIGNATURE   WITNESS SIGNATURE

THE CLERGY WELLNESS COMMISSION OF THE EPISCOPAL DIOCESE OF CALIFORNIA

Mission Statement
The Clergy Wellness Commission is a Commission of the Episcopal Diocese of California, composed of both clergy and laity.

The Mission Is . . .
to promote the health and wellness of clergy and their families,
to educate and encourage the growth of healthy congregations, and
to provide guidelines for both clergy and congregations alike to enable parishes to develop and maintain a healthy, open, generous workplace where the Holy Spirit is active and alive.

Our Premise
The guiding premise of the Clergy Wellness Commission is this: Healthy clergy make for healthy congregations and healthy congregations help create healthy clergy.

Our Functions
Goals and Objectives of the Commission:
• Educating clergy, families, and congregations about the nature of the stresses clergy face in ministry which can lead to burnout and dysfunctional behavior.
• Encouraging clergy and congregations to practice "Mutual Ministry" or "Total Ministry"—not where clergy are the only ministers "doing it all" but where clergy and laity have a shared ministry, in the church and in the world.
• Providing Diocesan guidelines and clear expectation to vestries in regards to maximum hours full-time clergy are expected to work and what diocesan standards are in terms of benefits, sick leave, vacation time, sabbatical time, continuing education, transportation reimbursements, and support for parental/family medical leave.
• Encouraging clergy and vestries to be mutually accountable to each other with the use of:
1. Work Agreements describing salary, full benefits, pension, self-employment tax support, sick leave, vacation time, sabbatical time, continuing education, and support for parental/family medical leave; and
2. Health Agreements made by clergy and negotiated with their vestry outlining ways in which clergy intend to maintain their spiritual, emotional, mental, and physical well-being and ways vestries can support them in this.

• Encouraging and educating clergy and vestries how to conduct "Mutual Ministry Reviews" (at least annually), which evaluate the strengths, growth areas, dreams, and goals of both clergy and vestries.
• Encouraging vestries to design appropriate job descriptions for all positions (lay and ordained) in church staffs and to provide samples.
• Providing an outline of a Mentoring Program for new clergy in the Diocese.
• Educating and clarifying to congregations the roles and stresses rectors, vicars, assistants, deacons, interim, retired, women, gay, and ethnic clergy face.

• Providing a bibliography and a list of resources for clergy and congregations in the Bay area and the wider church (through the internet) about wellness and developing healthy congregations.

Source: http://www.cwcdiocal.org/mission.html

The Resource Center for Pastoral Excellence at Samford University

The Resource Center for Pastoral Excellence at Samford University creates environments that foster pastoral excellence in the varied contexts of ministers from diverse backgrounds. The Center has three main emphases: Sabbath Opportunities and Resources, Pastor as Shepherd, and Pastoral Enrichment Network. *Sabbath Opportunities and Resources* provide restorative emotional, spiritual, physical, and intellectual experiences. Examples of resources offered include grants of financial support for ministerial sabbatical leaves and "Day Apart" retreats for women senior and solo pastors. *Pastor as Shepherd* provides nine-month peer support and learning opportunities for clergy groups. Offered in partnership with Birmingham's Samaritan Counseling Center, the program helps enhance pastoral ministry skills. *Pastoral Enrichment Network* provides facilitated peer support and group-directed continuing education for small groups of clergy located in rural communities, who lead smaller congregations.

For more information contact:

Michael Wilson, Program Director
Resource Center for Pastoral Excellence
Samford University
800 Lakeshore Drive
Birmingham, AL 35229

(205) 726-4064
www.samford.edu/rcpe
mkwilson@samford.edu

Other available titles from SMYTH & HELWYS®

Beyond the American Dream
Millard Fuller

In 1968, Millard finished the story of his journey from pauper to millionaire to home builder. His wife, Linda, occasionally would ask him about getting it published, but Millard would reply, "Not now. I'm too busy." This is that story. 978-1-57312-563-5 272 pages/pb **$20.00**

Blissful Affliction
The Ministry and Misery of Writing

Judson Edwards

Edwards draws from more than forty years of writing experience to explore why we use the written word to change lives and how to improve the writing craft. 978-1-57312-594-9 144 pages/pb **$15.00**

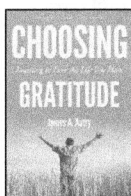

Choosing Gratitude
Learning to Love the Life You Have

James A. Autry

Autry reminds us that gratitude is a choice, a spiritual—not social—process. He suggests that if we cultivate gratitude as a way of being, we may not change the world and its ills, but we can change our response to the world. If we fill our lives with moments of gratitude, we will indeed love the life we have. 978-1-57312-614-4 144 pages/pb **$15.00**

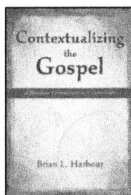

Contextualizing the Gospel
A Homiletic Commentary on 1 Corinthians

Brian L. Harbour

Harbour examines every part of Paul's letter, providing a rich resource for those who want to struggle with the difficult texts as well as the simple texts, who want to know how God's word—all of it—intersects with their lives today. 978-1-57312-589-5 240 pages/pb **$19.00**

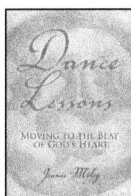

Dance Lessons
Moving to the Beat of God's Heart

Jeanie Miley

Miley shares her joys and struggles a she learns to "dance" with the Spirit of the Living God. 978-1-57312-622-9 240 pages/pb **$19.00**

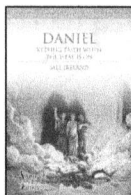

Daniel (Smyth & Helwys Annual Bible Study series)
Keeping Faith When the Heat Is On
Bill Ireland

Daniel is a book about resistance. It was written to people under pressure. In the book, we will see the efforts oppressive regimes take to undermine the faith and identity of God's people. In it, we will also see the strategies God's people employed in resisting the imposition of a foreign culture, and we will see what sustained their efforts. In that vein, the book of Daniel is powerfully relevant.

Teaching Guide 978-1-57312-647-2 144 pages/pb **$14.00**

Study Guide 978-1-57312-646-5 80 pages/pb **$6.00**

A Divine Duet
Ministry and Motherhood
Alicia Davis Porterfield, ed.

Each essay in this inspiring collection is as different as the mother-minister who wrote it, from theologians to chaplains, inner-city ministers to rural-poverty ministers, youth pastors to preachers, mothers who have adopted, birthed, and done both.

978-1-57312-676-2 146 pages/pb **$16.00**

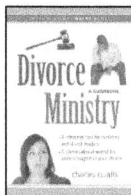

Divorce Ministry
A Guidebook
Charles Qualls

This book shares with the reader the value of establishing a divorce recovery ministry while also offering practical insights on establishing your own unique church-affiliated program. Whether you are working individually with one divorced person or leading a large group, *Divorce Ministry: A Guidebook* provides helpful resources to guide you through the emotional and relational issues divorced people often encounter.

978-1-57312-588-8 156 pages/pb **$16.00**

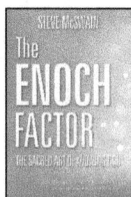

The Enoch Factor
The Sacred Art of Knowing God
Steve McSwain

The Enoch Factor is a persuasive argument for a more enlightened religious dialogue in America, one that affirms the goals of all religions—guiding followers in self-awareness, finding serenity and happiness, and discovering what the author describes as "the sacred art of knowing God."

978-1-57312-556-7 256 pages/pb **$21.00**

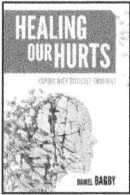

Healing Our Hurts
Coping with Difficult Emotions
Daniel Bagby

In *Healing Our Hurts*, Daniel Bagby identifies and explains all the dynamics at play in these complex emotions. Offering practical biblical insights to these feelings, he interprets faith-based responses to separate overly religious piety from true, natural human emotion. This book helps us learn how to deal with life's difficult emotions in a redemptive and responsible way. 978-1-57312-613-7 144 pages/pb **$15.00**

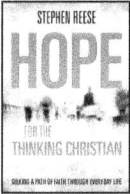

Hope for the Thinking Christian
Seeking a Path of Faith through Everyday Life
Stephen Reese

Readers who want to confront their faith more directly, to think it through and be open to God in an individual, authentic, spiritual encounter will find a resonant voice in Stephen Reese.

978-1-57312-553-6 160 pages/pb **$16.00**

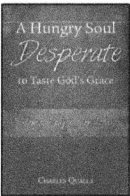

A Hungry Soul Desperate to Taste God's Grace
Honest Prayers for Life
Charles Qualls

Part of how we *see* God is determined by how we *listen* to God. There is so much noise and movement in the world that competes with images of God. This noise would drown out God's beckoning voice and distract us. Charles Qualls's newest book offers readers prayers for that journey toward the meaning and mystery of God. 978-1-57312-648-9 152 pages/pb **$14.00**

James M. Dunn and Soul Freedom
Aaron Douglas Weaver

James Milton Dunn, over the last fifty years, has been the most aggressive Baptist proponent for religious liberty in the United States. Soul freedom—voluntary, uncoerced faith and an unfettered individual conscience before God—is the basis of his understanding of church-state separation and the historic Baptist basis of religious liberty.

978-1-57312-590-1 224 pages/pb **$18.00**

The Jesus Tribe
Following Christ in the Land of the Empire
Ronnie McBrayer

The Jesus Tribe fleshes out the implications, possibilities, contradictions, and complexities of what it means to live within the Jesus Tribe and in the shadow of the American Empire.

978-1-57312-592-5 208 pages/pb **$17.00**

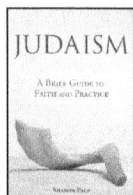

Judaism
A Brief Guide to Faith and Practice
Sharon Pace

Sharon Pace's newest book is a sensitive and comprehensive introduction to Judaism. What is it like to be born into the Jewish community? How does belief in the One God and a universal morality shape the way in which Jews see the world? How does one find meaning in life and the courage to endure suffering? How does one mark joy and forge community ties?

978-1-57312-644-1 144 pages/pb **$16.00**

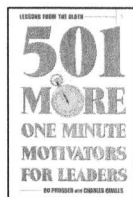

Lessons from the Cloth 2
501 More One Minute Motivators for Leaders
Bo Prosser and Charles Qualls

As the force that drives organizations to accomplishment, leadership is at a crucial point in churches, corporations, families, and almost every arena of life. Without leadership there is chaos. *With* leadership there is sometimes chaos! In this follow-up to their first volume, Bo Prosser and Charles Qualls will inspire you to keep growing in your leadership career.

978-1-57312-665-6 152 pages/pb **$11.00**

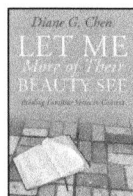

Let Me More of Their Beauty See
Reading Familiar Verses in Context
Diane G. Chen

Let Me More of Their Beauty See offers eight examples of how attention to the historical and literary settings can safeguard against taking a text out of context, bring out its transforming power in greater dimension, and help us apply Scripture appropriately in our daily lives.

978-1-57312-564-2 160 pages/pb **$17.00**

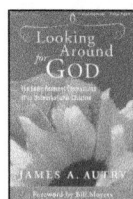

Looking Around for God
The Strangely Reverent Observations of an Unconventional Christian
James A. Autry

Looking Around for God, Autry's tenth book, is in many ways his most personal. In it he considers his unique life of faith and belief in God. Autry is a former Fortune 500 executive, author, poet, and consultant whose work has had a significant influence on leadership thinking.

978-157312-484-3 144 pages/pb **$16.00**

Maggie Lee for Good

Jinny and John Hinson

Maggie Lee for Good captures the essence of a young girl's boundless faith and spirit. Her parents' moving story of the accident that took her life will inspire readers who are facing loss, looking for evidence of God's sustaining grace, or searching for ways to make a meaningful difference in the lives of others.   978-1-57312-630-4 144 pages/pb **$15.00**

Making the Timeless Word Timely
A Primer for Preachers

Michael B. Brown

Michael Brown writes, "There is a simple formula for sermon preparation that creates messages that apply and engage whether your parish is rural or urban, young or old, rich or poor, five thousand members or fifty." The other part of the task, of course, involves being creative and insightful enough to know how to take the general formula for sermon preparation and make it particular in its impact on a specific congregation. Brown guides the reader through the formula and the skills to employ it with excellence and integrity.   978-1-57312-578-9 160 pages/pb **$16.00**

Meeting Jesus Today
For the Cautious, the Curious, and the Committed

Jeanie Miley

Meeting Jesus Today, ideal for both individual study and small groups, is intended to be used as a workbook. It is designed to move readers from studying the Scriptures and ideas within the chapters to recording their journey with the Living Christ.

978-1-57312-677-9 320 pages/pb **$19.00**

The Ministry Life
101 Tips for New Ministers

John Killinger

Sharing years of wisdom from more than fifty years in ministry and teaching, *The Ministry Life: 101 Tips for New Ministers* by John Killinger is filled with practical advice and wisdom for a minister's day-to-day tasks as well as advice on intellectual and spiritual habits to keep ministers of any age healthy and fulfilled.   978-1-57312-662-5 244 pages/pb **$19.00**

To order call **1-800-747-3016** or visit **www.helwys.com**

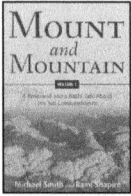

Mount and Mountain
Vol. 1: A Reverend and a Rabbi Talk About the Ten Commandments
Rami Shapiro and Michael Smith

Mount and Mountain represents the first half of an interfaith dialogue—a dialogue that neither preaches nor placates but challenges its participants to work both singly and together in the task of reinterpreting sacred texts. Mike and Rami discuss the nature of divinity, the power of faith, the beauty of myth and story, the necessity of doubt, the achievements, failings, and future of religion, and, above all, the struggle to live ethically and in harmony with the way of God.   *978-1-57312-612-0 144 pages/pb* **$15.00**

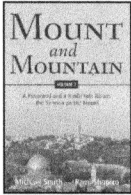

Mount and Mountain
Vol. 2: A Reverend and a Rabbi Talk About the Sermon on the Mount
Rami Shapiro and Michael Smith

This book, focused on the Sermon on the Mount, represents the second half of Mike and Rami's dialogue. In it, Mike and Rami explore the text of Jesus' sermon cooperatively, contributing perspectives drawn from their lives and religious traditions and seeking moments of illumination.   *978-1-57312-654-0 254 pages/pb* **$19.00**

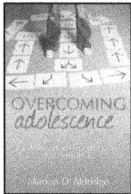

Overcoming Adolescence
Growing Beyond Childhood into Maturity
Marion D. Aldridge

In *Overcoming Adolescence*, Marion Aldridge poses questions for adults of all ages to consider. His challenge to readers is one he has personally worked to confront: to grow up *all the way*—mentally, physically, academically, socially, emotionally, and spiritually. The key involves not only knowing how to work through the process but also how to recognize what may be contributing to our perpetual adolescence.

978-1-57312-577-2 156 pages/pb **$17.00**

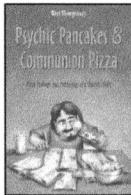

Psychic Pancakes & Communion Pizza
More Musings and Mutterings of a Church Misfit
Bert Montgomery

Psychic Pancakes & Communion Pizza is Bert Montgomery's highly anticipated follow-up to *Elvis, Willie, Jesus & Me* and contains further reflections on music, film, culture, life, and finding Jesus in the midst of it all.   *978-1-57312-578-9 160 pages/pb* **$16.00**

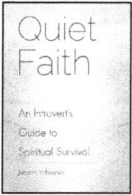

Quiet Faith
An Introvert's Guide to Spiritual Survival

Judson Edwards

In eight finely crafted chapters, Edwards look at key issues like evangelism, interpreting the Bible, dealing with doubt, and surviving the church from the perspective of a confirmed, but sometimes reluctant, introvert. In the process, he offers some provocative insights that introverts will find helpful and reassuring. *978-1-57312-681-6 144 pages/pb* **$15.00**

Reading Ezekiel (Reading the Old Testament series)
A Literary and Theological Commentary

Marvin A. Sweeney

The book of Ezekiel points to the return of YHWH to the holy temple at the center of a reconstituted Israel and creation at large. As such, the book of Ezekiel portrays the purging of Jerusalem, the Temple, and the people, to reconstitute them as part of a new creation at the conclusion of the book. With Jerusalem, the Temple, and the people so purged, YHWH stands once again in the holy center of the created world.

978-1-57312-658-8 264 pages/pb **$22.00**

Reading Job (Reading the Old Testament series)
A Literary and Theological Commentary

James L. Crenshaw

At issue in the Book of Job is a question with which most all of us struggle at some point in life, "Why do bad things happen to good people?" James Crenshaw has devoted his life to studying the disturbing matter of theodicy—divine justice—that troubles many people of faith.

978-1-57312-574-1 192 pages/pb **$22.00**

Reading Judges (Reading the Old Testament series)
A Literary and Theological Commentary

Mark E. Biddle

Reading the Old Testament book of Judges presents a number of significant challenges related to social contexts, historical settings, and literary characteristics. Acknowledging and examining these difficulties provides a point of entry into the world of Judges and promises to enrich the reading experience. *978-1-57312-631-1 240 pages/pb* **$22.00**

Reading Samuel (Reading the Old Testament series)
A Literary and Theological Commentary

Johanna W. H. van Wijk-Bos

Interpreted masterfully by preeminent Old Testament scholar Johanna W. H. van Wijk-Bos, the story of Samuel touches on a vast array of subjects that make up the rich fabric of human life. The reader gains an inside look at leadership, royal intrigue, military campaigns, occult practices, and the significance of religious objects of veneration.

978-1-57312-607-6 272 pages/pb **$22.00**

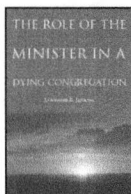

The Role of the Minister in a Dying Congregation

Lynwood B. Jenkins

Jenkins provides a courageous and responsible resource on one of the most critical issues in congregational life: how to help a congregation conclude its ministry life cycle with dignity and meaning.

978-1-57312-571-0 96 pages/pb **$14.00**

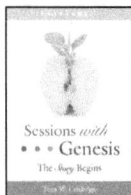

Sessions with Genesis (Session Bible Studies series)
The Story Begins

Tony W. Cartledge

Immersing us in the book of Genesis, Tony Cartledge examines both its major stories and the smaller cycles of hope and failure, of promise and judgment. Genesis introduces these themes of divine faithfulness and human failure in unmistakable terms, tracing Israel's beginning to the creation of the world and professing a belief that Israel's particular history had universal significance.

978-1-57312-636-6 144 pages/pb **$14.00**

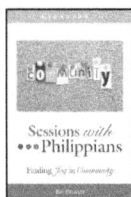

Sessions with Philippians (Session Bible Studies series)
Finding Joy in Community

Bo Prosser

In this brief letter to the Philippians, Paul makes clear the centrality of his faith in Jesus Christ, his love for the Philippian church, and his joy in serving both Christ and their church.

978-1-57312-579-6 112 pages/pb **$13.00**

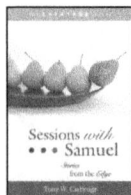

Sessions with Samuel (Session Bible Studies series)
Stories from the Edge

Tony W. Cartledge

In these stories, Israel faces one crisis after another, a people constantly on the edge. Individuals such as Saul and David find themselves on the edge as well, facing troubles of leadership and personal struggle. Yet, each crisis becomes a gateway for learning that God is always present, that hope remains.

978-1-57312-555-0 112 pages/pb **$13.00**

Silver Linings
My Life Before and After Challenger 7

June Scobee Rodgers

We know the public story of *Challenger 7*'s tragic destruction. That day, June's life took a new direction that ultimately led to the creation of the Challenger Center and to new life and new love. Her story of Christian faith and triumph over adversity will inspire readers of every age. *978-1-57312-570-3 352 pages/hc* **$28.00**

Spacious
Exploring Faith and Place

Holly Sprink

Exploring where we are and why that matters to God is an ongoing process. If we are present and attentive, God creatively and continuously widens our view of the world, whether we live in the Amazon or in our own hometown. *978-1-57312-649-6 156 pages/pb* **$16.00**

This Is What a Preacher Looks Like
Sermons by Baptist Women in Ministry

Pamela Durso, ed.

In this collection of sermons by thirty-six Baptist women, their voices are soft and loud, prophetic and pastoral, humorous and sincere. They are African American, Asian, Latina, and Caucasian. They are sisters, wives, mothers, grandmothers, aunts, and friends. *978-1-57312-554-3 144 pages/pb* **$18.00**

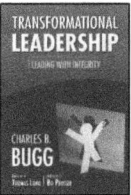

Transformational Leadership
Leading with Integrity

Charles B. Bugg

"Transformational" leadership involves understanding and growing so that we can help create positive change in the world. This book encourages leaders to be willing to change if *they* want to help transform the world. They are honest about their personal strengths and weaknesses, and are not afraid of doing a fearless moral inventory of themselves. *978-1-57312-558-1 112 pages/pb* **$14.00**

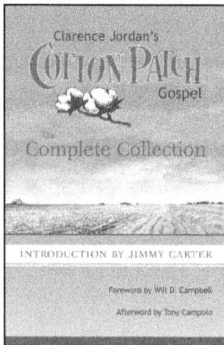

www.ingramcontent.com/pod-product-compliance
Lightning Source LLC
LaVergne TN
LVHW051747080426
835511LV00018B/3258